Notes To Stephanie:

Middle Aged Love Letters

And Life Stories

By

Jeffery W. Turner

Published in the USA

ISBN-13: 978-0-615-32352-7

Table Of Contents

Forward 7
One Day 10
Grey To White 11
Rilke Dragons 12
Our Sky 13
Forever 14
I Found This Picture 16
Valentines 001 17
Valentines 002 19
Valentines 003 21
Working As A Team 22
Forgiveness 24
Breakfast In Bed 26
Colors Of the Rainbow 28
Do You Ever Wonder? 30
Forks In The Road 32
When We Walk 34
Thoughts 36
Another Busy Weekend 39
Our Dance Step 41
Your Heart Was Torn Out 43
When Will Our Trials And Tribulations End? 46
The Recent Events 48

Your Interview Yesterday 50
The Story Unfolds 52
Good Friday And Easter 55
It's The Thought That Counts 57
Beads 59
More Beads 61
Family 64
Our Kids 66
Sweet Spot 68
Giving Your All 70
Adult Playtime 72
May 5th 74
Good Weekend 76
Liking Each Other 78
Our Trip 80
You Said You Had A Fear Of Being Left 82
Your Most Recent Interview 85
Dreams 87
Cabals And Clicks 90
The Ebb And Flow Of Life 92
Our Kids, Our Kids 95
Having Fun With Each Other 97
Dreading A Holiday Family Get Together 100
One Year Ago We Met 103

Once More Into The Breach Dear Friends........................105
Personalities 107
Almost Married One Year...109
What Will Our Families Think? 111
Do You Remember These Pictures? 114
Angst And Worry 116
New Beginnings 119
My Dear Competent Wife 121
Selling Yourself 123
Victory Against The Looming Threats...............................126
This Is The Kind Of Place 128
Rainy Days 131
Ahhhhh 133
An Unnamed Girl Is Sent Into the Cold............................135
Kids And Such 137
Finally...140
The Rain Today 142
Friday And Fun 144
And Yet We Now Gather 146
Another Year For Us Now Begins 148
Another Year Begins For Sure..151
A Woman Loved 153
A True Thanksgiving Awaits Us...155
My Darling Wife...158

A Bright Aurora 161

The Picture Above 163

The Christmas Season 165

And the Seasons Go Round And Round 167

Another New Year Has Begun 169

Well 171

That Song 173

Contract Day 175

Worried About My Mom 177

We Had A Good Weekend 179

It Has Been A While 182

Warmth And Heat 184

Our Talents 186

The Trip To See Jane 188

The Sadness One Feels 191

Surprises And Such 194

Christmas And Material Gifts 196

Christmas Family Gathering Angst 199

Another Year Is Upon Us 202

The Other Side Of the Sky 204

A Child's Frustration's 206

Disappointment 209

The Ghost Of Love Past 211

Afterward 214

Forward

What is this book you might be asking? It is a series of love notes and other kinds of notes I wrote on various life event subjects to a lady named Stephanie that I met and married. Many of these little tomes record things that happened to us as we rode down life's road. Some good, some bad as you will see. These types of things certainly appear in the lives of everyone over time. And this appeal is one reason I put them together in a book. The reader can no doubt substitute their name and family into many of these stories, all of which are true.

Returning to the notes themselves they are the story of our life together as middle aged adults with kids who are mostly grown up themselves. The notes cover our love, our tribulations, some defeats, and a few triumphs as well. The nature of life as an endless parade of varied events is something inherent to what I wrote as are the obvious stages and cycles of life itself like growing old and one's children leaving the proverbial nest to live their own lives filled with ups and downs.

You might also be wondering why I started writing them. That was sort of by accident. I was driving to work one day and was treated to a beautiful sunrise. I wrote about that which was the first note. Many of them were written on my lunch hour or on a break so many of them have a "stream of consciousness" feel to them. Also I never edited them except to clean up some typos and the grammar sometimes. Thus, the material you see is almost exactly as the originals were written. Over time they grew in size and frequency of creation. Some are short and some are as long as a couple of pages. There was no set frequency to when I wrote them and a few of the oldest ones I could not find.

So did Stephanie write any notes to me? Not per se, sometimes she would pen a short email reply to my notes, each of which we called an "ILYPANTS", but she did not write any corresponding body of notes related to mine. So this book is mostly my view of things that took place in our married life. By the way "ILYPANTS" stands for "I Love You Plus A Note To Stephanie".

Some of you will notice that in some of the notes I refer to a picture or an image which is not in the note in this book. The reason is that when I originally wrote them I would pull some image off of the net and put it at the top of the note. Since many of these images are copyrighted I removed them from this book. You can let your imagination form your own image when you read one of these notes.

You will see that I usually never go into any detail about the events in our life. The reason is simple. She and I knew the details; the notes were not to simply repeat what we knew but instead they were to reflect on what happened in some form with things like our life philosophies thrown in where it seemed to make sense. Also while many of the notes allude to a difficult time we had I never go into being harsh or overly critical about the people I am referring to. That was never the point of the notes.

To sum things up, the above paragraphs are why you see these notes here and how or why I wrote them over three years. I hope many of you can identify with the stories in them and also know how other "middle aged" adults and couples wrestle with the same things every day.

Jeff Turner, 9/12/2009.

Visit **www.ilypants.net** for more information.

One Day

I am, as you know, ready to walk with you down one of life's roads. *Or, is it a superhighway maybe?* And see what happens. We see the beginning of this journey, but its destination is not yet clearly seen. That place, tucked away in our hearts, is somewhere around a curve of life's unpredictable events, or on the other side of some steep emotional hills. Yet our minds know there is someplace where we want to arrive safe one day. So we will indeed see what time holds for us both under some unknown sky, hopefully filled with bright white clouds streaming over our two heads, while we stroll hand in hand one sunny day down life's path.

Jeff to Stephanie July 18, 2006

Grey To White

A great sunrise on the way in. There were some high cirrus clouds near the horizon. They were dark grey and featureless. As the sun started to rise, they changed from grey to blue, then pink, to finally bright white. This change is like some things in our lives that have happened. Things may at one time be dark and lonely, or stressful. But as time goes on, things get brighter and better. In the end all is well, especially when we are surrounded by the love and care of those who are special to us. A white and bright love like those perfect and spotless clouds in the eastern sky over-arching this Earth of ours. Together, we have that within us and our hearts. Our love spreads over us, binding us together under our own emotional sky.

Jeff to Stephanie, August 15, 2006

Rilke Dragons

"How should we be able to forget those ancient myths that are at the beginning of all peoples? The myths about dragons that at the last moment turn into princesses. Perhaps all the dragons of our lives are princesses, only waiting to see us once beautiful and brave. Perhaps everything terrible is, in its deepest being, something helpless that wants help from us. So you must not be frightened if a sadness rises up before you larger than any you have ever seen. If restiveness like light and cloud shadows passes over your hands and over all you, you must think that something is happening with you. That life has not forgotten you, that it holds you in its hand. It will not let you fall."

-- Maria Ranier Rilke, Letters To A Young Poet

Jeff To Stephanie, August 16, 2006

Our Sky

Walking together under an endless sky, across a never ending plain to a place unknown. This is life's journey, our walk taken to a place we sense in our hearts but cannot yet see. Looking across the distances of our lives, from those things both good and bad, and the things in between that fill most of our days, we can still be filled with excitement and hope. Hope for the things yet unseen below the horizon, or on the other side of a hill shimmering in the distance under the sun and clouds high overhead. Knowing there are many good things yet to come keeps us walking together, hand in hand underneath our own sky, the clouds our constant reminder of our love for each other, and of our trust in each other. They guide us to a place where we will rest easy over the years in each other's soft embrace.

Jeff To Stephanie, August 15, 2006

Forever

Forever. Remember that Saturday night you told me with such love and emotion in your eyes you wanted to be with me *forever*? I still think of that, the picture of you so clear in my mind filling me with strong emotions still.

You said that when we die our being, our soul, our energy leaves our body and goes off into the universe. You said you hoped we would be together then, forever, somehow our energy finding each other. Who knows what happens when we die. Maybe you are right. I surely hope so. Knowing you now, the corporeal Stephanie that I love so much, how could I bear to *not* be with you *forever*? It really does hurt to think of not having you around one day.

That hurt of someday not having you with me is a sign of how much I love you, and is a feeling that I have never had before with anyone. Your wish of never being apart from me shows clearly how much you really love me. The look of hope, love, and longing in your big, beautiful eyes when you said that still shines in my mind's eye just as bright as it did that evening in our den. Maybe it took all of our ups and downs over the years to know what real love is and how much it means to have it. And how much it would hurt to lose it.

Regardless of what eternity holds, I will always enjoy the time we have in this reality. So if one day we can be together in the "great beyond" I know we will be happy there too, just as we are happy now in this plane of existence.

Jeff to Stephanie, February 21, 2007

I Found This Picture

I found this picture yesterday. See the little speck of the truck way down the road? I like to think that represents you and I years from now, with the foreground being the present time of our lives. The broad prairie is the rich canvass of life that the universe has painted for us. We are traveling down life's road with each other to wherever it takes us together, and forever, in love. Not looking back but looking ahead to what is over the horizon. Certainly we have had a few bumps in the road from things like the kids, and other things in our past lives, but it has to smooth out sometime soon doesn't it? Yes, smooth like the road in the picture, and straight to where we want to go with our life together.

I hope we can get away one weekend soon and drive to someplace like that picture. Just you and me and some timeless space far away from the places of our daily life whose expanse will surround and swallow us, but give us rest from the things that have beset us so regularly since we wed almost four months ago.

Jeff To Stephanie, February 23, 2007

Valentines 001

I'm ready for many, many fun and happy Valentine's together with you too my Stephanie dear. Each succeeding one will be better than the last since we will have the memories of the ones previous to add to the one in the present with each other. Such times will enrich our love for each other and our life together as we get old. So one day when we wake up together and realize we are grey and wrinkled, it will be OK because we will have had many good times with one another. Valentines will be but one set of such memories that will fill our hearts and minds as the years unfold. The panorama of our experiences together will show everyone how a couple can be happy and enjoy each other without growing tired or weary of one another, even in the face of life's ups and downs and having a few eccentric personality traits.

Perhaps one day in a future that we can only dimly imagine our kids will realize that our love is a good thing and not something to see as a threat to their lifestyles, something to question, or be an object of their ridicule. But instead see it as something to aspire to have in their lives and remember fondly when they themselves are old and we are gone from this Earth of ours. Maybe one day in the twilight of their own lives, when they are thinking about us across the broad sea of decades long since past, they will realize they learned to love well by watching how happily and fully we loved each other.

Jeff to Stephanie, Valentine's Day 2007

Valentines 002

My dearest wife, friend, partner, and lover, I will always cherish you too. We will always walk hand in hand through the sometimes prickly garden of life. The sharp thorns of existence stick us but will not injure our love and affection for one another. To the contrary, such things will bring us closer together and strengthen our relationship that is now so young, so full of fire, and brimming with the spirit of life. Our garden of marriage will be like the spring time: green, bright, sunny, and warm. Not dark, cold, and barren like other gardens in life we have both been in. Truly, having seen landscapes that did not bring forth a rich harvest from life we both know that what we have sown through our love will provide a cornucopia of contentment. A Thanksgiving of the heart and soul will be ours, and is ours today in fact.

I know we will always be excited to be with each other and always long to see each other every day we are together across the years to come. I look forward to the rest of our lives with each other, regardless of the ups and downs that surely will be there. Traveling across these bumps, and also smooth places, in the highway of life are what define existence and reality itself. Regardless, such a journey will be the greatest trip we have ever taken. And the most fun, the most satisfying, the most comforting, and the most fulfilling. So I am ready to saunter on with you too down the road we have decided to walk down together.

Jeff To Stephanie, The Day After Valentines 2007

Valentines 003

Well now my love, we are a week past Valentines now and we still know we love each other as before. Somehow I know that the passage of time will not lessen or dull our sharp affection for each other. While we are still learning about each other's personalities, we still know what we knew all along: "I always loved you, I love you now, and I will always love you". Those words, spoken at our little wedding, ring true even now in our hearts.

That permanency of love is such a simple idea but yet it is so important to us both. Inside of us, we feel comfortable with each other and realize we will always feel that way. That certainty brings peace to our hearts as we live our lives and deal with its challenges. Many couples never know how that feels but we have it and will not lose that emotional warmth, or the closeness it has brought into our lives.

So now my wonderful, true Valentine and wife, I do love you so very much. And I know you love me the same way. This true commonality of feelings will make us one for as long as we live on this Earth. As will the words above that we spoke so truly at our wedding last Halloween.

Jeff to Stephanie, a week after Valentines 2007

Working As A Team

Working as a team. You are so right my dear; we really do work well together on many things as you said this morning in the kitchen (in between hugs and terms of endearment said with smiles and emotions to each other in our hurry to get to work). Like climbing up on the roof of your house Sunday to fix the roof damage after the big wind and dust storm on Saturday. We held the ladder and trusted one another. And had a good time after we were done surveying the view from up there. A small reward for trusting each other and working with that trust.

So many times since we have been together we went right to it on stuff we had to do. Like working to some unspoken project plan, we simply seem to blend together on tasks and to dos in many areas. And on many things in our lives. We seem to more and more know what the other is thinking and know what to do to keep things moving, don't we?

Surely that is one sign that we are good together, and meant for one another. If we were not comfortable with each other, and each other's way of doing things, we could not have done what we did this last weekend. As you said we have a yin-yang with each other.

That is what a marriage should have at its core. It is at the core of ours certainly. Something many marriages do not have. Certainly it is something new for both us, and we both see that. And we both appreciate having such a good thing, like other aspects of our relationship that more than make up for some of the bad quirks we both have and sometimes show. Therefore, let the good always triumph over the bad, and let the past be forgotten and be forgiven always, in favor of letting our teamwork make our present and our future always bright and good with each other forever.

Jeff to Stephanie February 26, 2007

Forgiveness

Forgiveness. Yes forgiveness is a two way street my darling. We must forgive each other but also ourselves. It is obvious that both of us sometimes have hurt the other through our fault driven actions. But also, we hurt ourselves by blaming ourselves for things that have happened to us or to our children. Now if we had done things deliberately to each other, or to our kids, or even to ourselves, to cause hurt then forgiveness would be a difficult thing to justify. But in our case, our mistakes were just that, mistakes. Not premeditated actions intent on hurting others.

Also, until time passes, just how does one know if something was a mistake sometimes? After the time a decision is made, the correctness of the path it dictated may later come into doubt by the appearance of new information or more wisdom. Things that one day seemed to be the logical may later become inexplicable.

Because it is impossible to exactly know if an action is really the correct thing to do, one has to forgive one's self for things that are later found to be mistakes. If you don't, you could judge your whole life to be a failure or a source of woe to yourself or to others.

Yes we will all fall short, as we both have, but in the end our hearts are true and our intentions good to ourselves and others. Since we are good people we have to be able to forgive each other and just as importantly ourselves. To do otherwise would mean forever suffering angst about what might have been done better instead of learning from our shortcomings and applying that hard earned knowledge to improve our lives by making better choices. So we must always tell ourselves the past is both gone and our actions were OK and move on down the road of life with better directions for the journey that will unfold along its length. That way, we will make fewer wrong turns at its forks.

Jeff To Stephanie, February 27, 2007

Breakfast In Bed

In the last few mornings we have been having our coffee, juice, and some food together in our bed before we get dressed. When you think about this, a couple having breakfast in bed is not that common, especially during the week. So what does this mean my dear?

I think it is one more sign that you and I really love each other and enjoy each other's company. And what few things do we NOT enjoy doing together? In short we like doing just about everything together. We are the type of couple that rarely goes off and does things on our own without considering the other.

I for one like doing things with you and I know you feel the same way towards me. It really has not mattered what we have done has it? Working at the rent house, cleaning our house, or doing laundry, you name it, we do it together. We are two people that are seemingly inseparable.

There are many, many worse things than being absorbed with each other and being inseparable isn't there? It is very strange that some people we know think that our intense love is a problem.

If our love for each another is a problem, it is a good problem to have. It is a something every couple should want to experience.

Jeff To Stephanie, February 28, 2007

Colors Of the Rainbow

Colors of the rainbow. You have more than one time my dear compared our personalities to the colors of the rainbow. A visible spectrum of behavior if you will. You said you were, and saw, the whole spectrum of light. Thus you saw people and events with more shades of grey than I did. While I was the mostly the ends: black and white. But with a ray of red down the middle, thus explaining my usual tendency of having one way or the other views but also showing why I have an almost inexplicable off the wall side (like my weird sense of humor) that cropped up from time to time.

Our personalities are therefore alike but yet different still. We share some colors, but many we do not. There is much we have in common but there are still enough differences to create great interest in the other and sometimes great frustration as well. These differences, and common traits, also ferment great passion in our love life and create a sense of wonder about the other most days.

In nature, a rainbow appears after a storm. It is luminous and shiny after the dark and rainy event that gave birth to it. Likewise with each of us, events both dark and stormy, but also ones that are bright and full of life, have made us who we are individually, and in turn who we are together as a couple.

The colors of our relationship rainbow really do blend together to create a close and exciting marriage that is also full of contentment, safety, and predictability for both of us. That way, as life's storms do rage around us, and the rainbows appear, we are consistent in our love for one another always.

Jeff To Stephanie February 28, 2007

Do You Ever Wonder?

Do you ever wonder what lies over the side of a hill? Underneath a cloud? Beyond the horizon and the curve of the world itself? Or wonder who lies underneath such sights as you gaze at them?

On a wintry day with high cirrus clouds streaming in from the west or the southwest, the visible curve of those clouds stretches back for maybe a hundred miles. Who lives under the overarching stream of whiteness? What towns are there? Whose lives are unfolding there? Seeing such things and thinking about who or what lies there gives me a sense of wonder and excitement that is hard to explain, but is there as sure as I tell you about it here.

And underneath the clouds high up and far away from where our lives unfold, do the people there look up as I do and wonder who or what lies underneath their distant sky? Underneath everyone's skies are people like you and me, living and hopefully loving.

Most people go about their daily lives largely unaware of who else is looking up and out at such scenes. But there are some of us who do notice the unfolding beauty high above and gain a rich sense of being alive as its bright curve of whiteness reaches around the larger node of existence and covers the wide arc of greater life-realities beneath it. Our lives forever enriched by the wonders unfolding above and beyond our own world-line.

Jeff To Stephanie February 28, 2007

Forks In The Road

Forks in the road of life. Many times my love we have asked ourselves "why did we meet each other?". We certainly do not think it was Divine Intervention or destiny after all. Since we are both pretty logical in our outlook on things, there must be some another reason than that. I think very simply it is the cumulative effect of all of the choices we have ever made across the years. They came together in June of 2006 when we met and fell in love.

It is like coming to an intersection with two routes one can take. You have to choose one way alone; you can't go down both roads at once. Nor can you know for sure where each road, and each choice in life, will take you. But you keep making turns and eventually get somewhere based on those changes in direction.

Some choices are in the end strewn with negative things. Like the lightning bolt in the picture hitting one fork in the highway. Except in life we don't know where the lightning will hit in advance most of the time. So without knowing it we take a turn for the worse, so to speak.

Sometimes we make a choice that in the end is

good. As with the bad routes in life, we don't know they are good until after we make the decision. Like going down the other fork in the road, there might not be lightning visible, but we don't know there is a better destination until we travel on for a bit further.

Over the decades of our lives we have made both types of turns, some good and some bad. Across the years of being alone, we hoped we would reach the safe destination of someone who would love us as we wanted to love. But we never knew when we would reach that spot on the road. In the end, we dodged enough of the lightning bolts on the wrong turns and instead made the right turns that brought us into each other's arms. And there we shall stay, safe at this milepost on life's road, our loving marriage to each other.

Jeff To Stephanie, February 27, 2007

When We Walk

When we walk do you notice all of the things we do? We hold hands, we walk arm in arm, we talk, and we smile at each other. Have you noticed what other couples do that we see when strolling in the park? Not the same things at all. They don't seem to hold hands, be affectionate, or do the other non-verbal things we seem to do all of the time. Clearly many of them talk as we do, but most do not act we do.

What does this mean do you think? Have they all been married so long that being affectionate is something they don't do? Do they so dislike each other that being physically close is an anathema to them? Or are they simply not the affectionate types at all? When I see other people and note their behavior I wonder what they are like many times. Do they hope and love like we do? Are they in some pattern where doing a simple thing like holding their mate's hands is something that never crosses their minds? Or are their lives so filled with despair that even though they have a mate or important person under the same roof with them they show no happiness or love to others?

I have many questions about the others I see but I possess few answers about them. While what our neighbors do and why they act the way they do is not something I know much for sure about, I do know why we do the things we do in the park, at home, and everywhere we go. We simply love each other a whole lot.

Yes, as my daughter somewhat derisively observed, we are absorbed with one another aren't we? This almost single minded focus on each other is why we hold hands, and walk arm in arm in the park, and can constantly talk to each other about any number of topics. I trust we will always be this way. It is a shame so many people we see do not seem to walk this happy path with their mates as we do.

Jeff To Stephanie March 1, 2007

Thoughts

Family is hard to deal with dearest. The ties that bind are also the ties that can cause the most hurt due to their closeness and intensity. A stranger does not afford such links, thus the hurt from a stranger is less.

With your kids and communicating with them, perhaps some distance from them is the best course right now. Let them cool off and adjust to not being able to hit the speed dial to mom's emotions and pocket book, especially since they do not respond to your attempts to have a normal relationship with them.

This is hard on you and I understand why. But you also cannot always stay tied up in knots emotionally about what they do or don't do. Simply because they will choose what they will do vis a vis you and I on their own. They obviously hold resentment towards you on more than one level, but there is nothing you can do about that either. You provided a lot for them and were there for them as a mother. As adults they at some point have to move on from their grievances towards you and live and let live. No parent is ever perfect and the kids sure aren't. The passage of time, garnering some real world experience, and some mature reflection on their parts will be necessary for this to happen.

As far as some of their bad behaviors, like your daughter's lack of honesty, you can't make her be like you. She is grown up and in her own world now, and has been for some time now. Some people will always deceive, while others can change when the consequences of such a path affects them. Where she is on this continuum is unknown.

"Son" is acting mad of course, but part of his path is simply him asserting his manhood, telling you he does not need you, even though he wishes perhaps for the old parasitic way of doing things. It is true you may never be close to him in the future but I do not think he forever will have no contact with you. In the end you cannot control their behavior, therefore you should not waste your mental energy and emotions trying to figure out why they don't act like you or I do.

And you have to let yourself live too darling. You and I have a pretty happy life together. Regardless of what everyone else does, we have to have our life too. You can't hold the past against yourself, nor can you change your kids to be in your own image as you might wish. You do have the power, and every right, to be happy and content with yourself and me. So I would say make the statements to your kids about contact and the like as we discussed earlier and see what happens. And until you see what transpires, you and I will live "happily ever after" with each other and do our own thing, just like everyone else is doing it seems.

Jeff To Stephanie March 2, 2007

Another Busy Weekend

Another very busy weekend is now done and we are back to work my dearest. And it was a good weekend; we got a lot of things done. And we did have some time to ourselves in between things. Especially Sunday morning and midday Sunday (Mrrroooowww !!!! We <CENSORED> THREE times....). Well, I digress as usual. But onward to more significant, and public, discussions now.

The point of my ramblings is that as we ourselves discussed, we enjoyed each other's company while doing work and chores. The highlight of these things was of course "The Sunday Odyssey On Our Roof". Yes, doing roof repairs can be something fun when done together. That one thing shows something wonderful about our relationship as we observed more than once in our almost un-ceasing talks the last two days and before. That is, we really like being with each other pretty much all of the time and can turn even the obvious drudgery and tedium of repairs and chores into something we can enjoy with one another.

Certainly another sign, actually proof, that we are absorbed with one another isn't it? I, for one, do not mind being this way. It is wonderful and shows what a marriage can be. Even at our "advanced" age, right? Each of us is a "Veteran of the Psychic Wars" (a Blue Oyster Cult song whose title I have used to refer to those of us who have "fought" in the "wars" of middle aged adult dating). But we have survived the tribulations of that emotional battlefield and can enjoy each other in most any setting.

Unlike many adult couples our age. And we also have endured all of the trials life has thrown at us since we most happily got married last Halloween. As Martha Stewart (who you like and who I despise) says "it's a good thing". On this one subject I will happily agree with Martha. But I won't buy her towels and sheets.

Jeff To Stephanie March 5, 2007

Our Dance Step

Hmmm....practicing our two-step before going dancing on St. Patrick's Day, especially since you never have danced in your whole life for all practical purposes. In a way this is like being in a relationship you know. We try some different things until we get it right for both of us.

Learning the detailed cadence of a dance step is like making a relationship work. A two-step, which to me is more like a four step, has a repeated set of specific movements. Each unique dance has its own cadence which is judged to be right. And likewise each relationship ultimately has its own set of steps too I think. The hard part about relationships is that there is really no pre-set cadence to know in advance. Yes, there are the things that any counselor or book on the subject will tell you to do to dance right with your partner, but in the end you really have to find out what works with each other on your own life's dance floor.

Therefore my dearest, since we will have to practice our two-step as is shown on that DVD I bought for us before we go out to the Rodeo Exchange Club on St. Patrick's Day, we also have to practice what makes us tick as one couple in our marriage won't we? Certainly it is an on-going series of lessons, just like what will be needed for us to even successfully do the basic two-step without looking like two uncoordinated tree sloths dressed in western finery.

But sort of like I said in my email on practicing for St Patty's Day dancing, practicing within our marriage ballroom will be as fun as practicing to go out on a real dance floor so to speak. I look forward to the steps and twirls with you over the days and years to come. In the end "practice makes perfect" doesn't it?

Jeff To Stephanie March 8, 2007

Your Heart Was Torn Out

Your heart has been torn out. Yes dearest it has been ripped out by the seemingly never ending transition with your kids, and also by my two yesterday. Regardless, these turn of events, well most of them anyway, would have happened whether or not we had ever met and married you know. If you had been by yourself, or had met someone else, the current state of affairs with your kids and their non-communication would have come to past. It was inevitable given their behavior and the necessity of protecting yourself from their seemingly usurious, parasitical ways. In order for you to have a life of your own you had to make your kids realize they had to take responsibility for their own lives and not expect you to facilitate whatever lifestyle they wished to pursue. This process is something that all parents must face in some measure as their hatchlings leave the nest to fly out on their own. Regardless of whether or not the mother bird pushed them out or they flew off by themselves.

Much of the hurt you feel is of course from the fact that your kids are your only real blood-kin on this earth. Now that we are married you have family by the event of taking our wedding vows. But your kids are still your only true blood relatives.

That makes the ties to them more strong and intense than those in most people's lives, including my own. That intensity has created much of the on-going hurt you have felt and still feel in your big, wonderful heart. This is normal and is very understandable. The time it will take to resolve this pain could be lengthy. That too is normal and something easy for me to comprehend.

Even with the emotional pain you feel stabbing at your being now, you know you have someone who loves you in your life, me of course. This is part of you being able to have your own life independent of how your kids apparently expected you to live alone and yet be at their beck and call for some indeterminate time. There is nothing wrong at all with you having your own life and existence. That too is normal. The angst your kids and mine feel toward our marriage is not something that should have bearing on our relationship per se. Yes, we should be there for our kids, but not at the cost of an emotional bar tab that never gets closed out.

Or at the cost of financial ruin either. You were being pushed into a corner where both of those costs were looming over you. You had to act and you did.

Now finally, you too can live a life that is full in a

normal, fun, and healthy marriage with someone who loves you and gives you love back in the abundant manner you yourself always freely gave to others, especially to your kids.

Jeff To Stephanie March 12, 2007

When Will Our Trials And Tribulations End?

So just when will our trials and tribulations end my Stephanie? This week has brought us yet another challenge with our kids to deal with. It is fortunate we do have some possible answers to this dilemma, but the answers are not perfect ones. At least this week's kid giving us heartburn is safe and OK, that we can be very thankful for. It seems to be another link in a chain of woe for us doesn't it? Oh well, perhaps God or life is punishing us for the crime of loving each other.

I think not. Life just throws people curve balls you know, the pitcher of probability, luck, and the choices of others keeps us playing past the ninth inning so to speak. Many times these things come in groups it seems; at least that is what I have seen in life over the years. Wave after wave of trouble and ire, then followed at some point by calm and peace. We just don't know when the high tide of stress will finally ebb away from our battered shores.

So far, you and I have weathered these mighty storms fairly well. Yes we have been affected by it all in ways that are not so good. You get forgetful, I snap at you. In spite of these shortcomings we do still have the ability to find the solutions to these problems and still love each other. This tells me we are both strong people capable of enduring much: things that might wilt or melt others with lesser strength away into a pool of depression or failure. Not us, we keep soldiering on amidst life's constant artillery barrage.

Yet I am still a bit tired of being on the front lines my dear. I would like some relief and R&R for us both away from this battlefield. That time will come for us, I just do not know when. Until our relief column comes we will just have to tighten our helmets and prepare for the worst and hope for the best. To do otherwise would be unlike us. That is why we have remained who we are over the years regardless of some inglorious defeats and setbacks, but also amongst brilliant victories like marrying each other.

Jeff To Stephanie March 14, 2007

The Recent Events

The recent events with your son made me want to repeat some things I have told you many times before. In short, we have to live our own lives regardless of what any of our kids do dear. Neither of us can control what they think or do since they are grown up. They are adults now (except for my daughter and she will be there too soon enough). Like us, our kids can do what they want when they want, and think what they want. The time in our lives for us to directly influence their existence is now over. Accordingly, we both must always keep that in mind and adjust our own actions and perceptions to recognize that new reality.

Even though both of our nests are now empty, mine having been empty for a long time obviously, it does not mean that our lives are empty. Far from it, you and I now have the ability, within reason of course, to really do what we want. Yes, you and I are not prone to doing stuff that is bad, or dangerous, or stupid, but we can live our day to day lives around each other. We can enjoy each other and look forward to our middle aged years and beyond. This is how it should be. At this point in our lives we can't stay up all night worrying about what our kids are doing. They are not worrying about what we are doing, that is for sure. So we can't be overly focused on trying to know what they are up to. Trying to do such a thing would be futile and it would not provide any benefit to us either.

We now have to be mostly spectators to the lives of our kids. It is up to them to make their lives good or bad. Just like it is up to us to make our life and marriage together a good one. In this we have mostly succeeded I think. We do love and enjoy each other even around a few spats. In this light I would say we are pretty typical for a couple of middle aged parents teetering on the brink of being grandparents one day (hopefully one year actually). Being typical is a good thing I say. Let's keep it that way, shall we?

Jeff To Stephanie March 23, 2007

Your Interview Yesterday

Some thoughts on your interview yesterday. Well, I will say again that you accrue no negative entries to your career account at all my Stephanie. At the very worst you are on their scope for Greater Things. Indeed the politics probably made the outcome preordained. But that is OK; many times things go like that in organizations. Such a dynamic is simply part of the flow of things when a group of people interact in some organization whether or not it is in business, or in education, or in higher academia.

Even though they want the other lady, they now cannot ignore your qualifications or claim that they do not know what you are capable of providing for the district. In fact the opposite is true now. Since people in the administration know now what your management at Mowder knows, this will facilitate you obtaining a vice principal or principal job when one turns up. Given that the test scores of your kids are good, that will also help you. Along with your other triumphs like being President of the Site Management Committee. All in all you have all of the ingredients for success at the district.

Therefore, I would say keep being patient. They like you and more people now know what you can do at the district. They know what I have known for a long time. That is, Stephanie Celeste Turner is a very capable and knowledgeable lady who is bound to accomplish great things for the kids she serves each day, doing so with a smile on her face and with dedication each day. I am behind you 100% in your quest to do more and better things.

Jeff To Stephanie March 27, 2007

The Story Unfolds

Now, in the recent past a series of events with your kids has shown that over time things generally will work themselves out. Before the last couple of weeks, it seemed to you that your kids were having nothing to do with you. In fact anyone would most likely think that due to their non-communication or near lack of communication with you. This of course hurt you a lot. I could see that clearly in your mood, your tone, and you waking up in the middle of the night talking about all of this. However, things have changed.

Your daughter started talking to you more. Yes, she came over asking for stuff of course and wanted you to drop what you were doing to do stuff with her without consideration for what you were doing, but in the end she is talking to you more regularly. Of course she has to realize there are some new rules shall we say due to our marriage and her past errors, but she is talking and coming over. Those are good things indeed.

Now Son's latest disasters have had a positive side too. He will talk on the phone some now, and he came over for dinner. It seems the ice has been broken with him too and perhaps he is starting to assume responsibility for his actions and grow up. And his new job looks to be something that he also needs and might be very good for him. All of this in the end is good for him and you. You are more at ease and relaxed when you know that he is well.

In my heart I felt that over time these issues would be resolved with your kids realizing that you too have a life and that you were not responsible for enabling their desires to live like adults. Kind of like the old cliché "time heals". It may be a cliché and trite in its sound, but in the end there is a lot of truth to the saying. Indeed, time and events have changed the dynamic between you and your brood. No doubt time and other events will also affect my two kids and how they deal with us and me individually as their dad. That story has yet to be written of course, and the story about you and your children is also still being told. Both of these epic tales will unfold over the course of our entire lives, and beyond after we are gone. All of us have our own tale to tell you know, sometimes surrounded by a cast of characters like our kids and parents, the actors for life's play are all around us. One day our kids may be trying to see how the story of their own children will turn out, hopefully guided by what was written for them by life, lessons learned, and us over the long trail of years. Like us, they too will wonder if there will be a happy ending or not to the drama at hand. And maybe talk for hours in the middle of the night to their spouses like we have. Thus, the never ending story, the cycle of life and family, will continue across the years to come.

Jeff To Stephanie March 30, 2007

Good Friday And Easter

Will it be a *Good* Friday for us tomorrow my love? The past few days have been a bit difficult as you know, but I am going to say it WILL be a *Good* Friday for us tomorrow. The reason should be clear to us both. We simply love each other in spite of our individual faults. Therefore one can compare that aspect of our relationship to the events associated with Good Friday and on this upcoming Easter.

Good Friday, the day of the crucifixion, could be compared to some of our hard times and fusses, each with the hope of reconciliation symbolized by the forgiveness of the Cross. Easter and its resurrection could be seen as our ultimate kissing and making up after a fuss, or the relief or resolution of some hard issue we have had to face such as some of the stuff with our brood of kids. So even though neither us is really religious in the sense we were grew up in and later drew away from, we can see parallels in that religious symbology in our life together can't we?

Well, I have no desire to literally squirm naked on some cross surrounded by two thieves, but I can say we have endured some things like that figuratively speaking. And also we have also have had a resurrection in a conceptual sense as well. Looking at some of the things over the years we have been through, especially in your life, we could say that like Christ we have arisen from the dead so to speak by finding our life and love together, haven't we? More than once in fact; which would not be a strictly Biblical parallel.

But when are you and I strictly religious or purely conventional after all? If we were, we would not be you and I would we? I'll take what we are now as a couple, and "worship" that as opposed to the dogmatic what ifs of conventional religion any day of the week.

Jeff To Stephanie April 5, 2007

It's The Thought That Counts

Today, you calling me and simply telling me you loved me, and a couple of other things, was such a wonderful little, but so important thing to do my dear. In the lives and relationships of so many people, I feel that many folks simply lose sight of the fact that actions like that, not things, make such an important difference to someone.

Indeed, I give you flowers which are things, but also, the time spent to do that for you is just as important, and is really more important and significant I think.

Why one might ask? Very simply it is like the saying "it's the thought that counts". Yes it is the thought because that shows what is truly inside of someone, not the result of the action derived from a thought. Your quick but thoughtful call on your way into Mowder was a small but yet very large thing. That action came from a thought that came from your love for me that sits deep inside of your heart and your very soul. That shows truly how you feel about me and I notice such things above all else that you do for me.

So when you called you really made my day my Stephanie, you really did. That shows me that regardless of how busy you are, or what you are doing, that I am on your mind and in your heart. And I want you to know that I truly love you too, every time I call or email you during the work day I am expressing the same heartfelt love for you that you did for me just a few minutes ago while I sat eating my lunch. And just think my dearest wife, friend, and lover girl; it will be my turn to call you in a just a little bit so I can return the love you just showed me.

Jeff To Stephanie April 4, 2007

Beads

Remember the line in the movie Forrest Gump that said "life is like a box of chocolates"? To me it seems life is really like a string of your beads.

Each bead is some event in our lives. They look different, just like each thing in our life is different to an extent. The string or wire you use to put them on is the linear progression of time. The beads line up from the start to the end just like the events in our lives unfolds one after another from the time we are born until we pass on.

Some of the beads are shiny and smooth and others are rough and irregular. Some are made of precious stone, others from plastic or wood. Some are cheap on the outside but plated with something more valuable on the surface. In a similar way, the things that happen to us as we live also vary in their makeup and content. Our lives are filled with the pretty, the cheap, the bad, and the precious don't you know. We both have experienced a plethora of such things across the years of our lives, the long fully beaded wire or string that is our existence.

While many times we are given the beads to put on our life's wire, sometimes pretty, cheap, or precious, we do have some choice as to what to put on our personal strings. In that light, we can say we together chose the same precious stone to string when we fell in love and decided to marry each other.

Yes, in our life together there are some cheap beads, and some bad ones too, but all in all the fine and precious prevail in our new life together. To ourselves and the people we know, we are adorned with finery, our life strands intertwined by the bright glitter of our feelings for each other. Thus, the pretty panoply of our love for each other is shown to all. That fact is something we can treasure and appreciate each day regardless of the type of beads we are given, or choose, to wear upon our lives' long strands.

Jeff To Stephanie April 19, 2007

More Beads

And how the beads are strung together is another thought in and of itself my darling. There is a wide assortment of beads you can put together on a wire or a string to make something. You lay out many possibilities and combine the shapes and colors into a design that is pleasing to you. Maybe a pattern that is pleasing to others like me too.

Regardless of one's inventory of beads and the related accoutrements, you are making a choice each time you pick up a bead and put it next to one on a string or a wire. One conscious choice to make for one's self out a nearly endless array of possibilities. In the end however, you can only make one choice for a bead to put on a string or a wire.

Life is like that too. In general, we choose the type of life we will lead. Things like the career we follow or whether or not to have children or marry. Those types of choices form the wire or string of our lives. If we had chosen differently, the string we have now would be very different. Think how many times in each of our lives we could have chosen differently, each choice we did make formed the string we now wear around ourselves. Like how we met, it was culmination of many choices across our whole adult lives. In the end, it formed the wire we now wear with each other in marriage.

Once we have the string we of course have the beads of our daily lives to put upon it too. Each day we choose beads, both pretty and not so pretty to put on the string we have made for ourselves. When we make love or spend happy times together we are using the precious stones, the turquoise of love and adoration for each other so to speak. When we fuss or irritate the other we have chosen some cheap imitation. All of these beads create the colors and shapes of our everyday lives strung out on the string our earlier choices made. Our daily moods, pleasures, and woes come forth from what type of bead we reach for. The different shapes and colors flash at us and also show others how we are living.

In the end, I know we choose the pretty beads most of the time. Yes, we also pick some ugly ones too. That combination makes us who we are individually and who we are as a couple. That design and pattern is always being added to, something that is never finished, ever evolving to a greater form of beauty that we both can admire and enjoy.

At least as long as we both are upon this Earth. And who knows maybe beyond this world too if we are lucky. I guess we will not know the answer to that last question until the final bead is strung and all of the little bags of beads they now fill, each beckoning us to choose from, are empty.

Jeff To Stephanie April 19, 2007

Family

One of your great wishes when we were dating and engaged was to be part of an extended family again. We discussed that in detail and that is perhaps the biggest reason we got married on Halloween as opposed to waiting for a time after that. You really never had that in your life, even with Gigi et al, and it was obviously a missing link in what you wanted out of your life.

Now that we are married you do have that. You can see that obviously in how you and my mom get along. She has shown you things and told you stories no one but family has been. But that is the point my love, you are family now. Part of a bigger family than just you and me, or you and your two children (who I consider my own now too). Indeed, the Turner family has had its ups and downs as you know, but the core of my mom, my sister, and I remain. Now you too are part of that core, that galactic center of the stars that make up the constellation of our family. You are new to the family by our recent marriage but I think you can see now that my mom treats you like long time blood kin. She enjoys and respects you, and you her. That shows you are part of the clan, perhaps more than you realize now.

In regards to our four kids, you rightly point out that we will be the core of that part of the Turner universe one day. Or should I say Turner/Long universe? Regardless of the parental lineage of our children, one day when we are old we will be what remain, ignoring of course my sister and her children for this discussion. At that time we will have our sons and daughters in law, and our grandchildren to watch and enjoy. Hopefully, we will be able to share many stories from our lives with them just as my mom has shared such things with you and of course my sister and I over the years. I wish my dad was still here; he too would have loved you and shared a few tales of his own with you.

Thus, as who is the center of a family changes as the generations grow up, age, and finally die, the continuity of our family, which you and your kids now grace, will go on over the years and decades now unseen. Perhaps the stories we will one day tell to our various descendents will be the best legacy we can leave to them. Hopefully things with insight and meaning that will be more valuable to them than any monetary inheritance we could bequeath in our passing. And hopefully they will do the same when they are the center of their own wider clans.

Jeff to Stephanie April 23, 2007

Our Kids

Our kids. Well this weekend was a time for seeing what some of our kids are up to wasn't it? From Jane's prom to Jimmy's B-day. Certainly, we can see that all of our children are unique, as they should be as they grow up. The point however of this note is not that they are growing up but even though we are mostly passive spectators to their lives now, we can see that the passage of time many time produces results that are positive without our direct intervention.

In Son's case, he seems to be seeing things more and more from an adult perspective, like recognizing how much time you spent cleaning up after him now that he was cleaning up after Heather's invasive pets.. Such experiences, both large and small, are the events that cause someone to grow up aren't they?

In Jane's case, we see how grown up she is now at 17 years of age. She looks like a young woman now and many times acts like one too. We shall see if she remains level headed in the face of her on-going romance with Jamie: a long term romance is another life experience that makes one grow up and learn how to act like an adult. Time will tell on this situation since we certainly are spectators to that ballgame.

And who knows when Cynthia or Roger will next need us for something? Probably sooner that we expect.

So again, we now watch from a far shore so to speak, and see our kids becoming adults and sailing away from us on their own life's voyages. At the same time we can navigate our own sea together without feeling guilty about the lack of the day to day presence of our kids under our own roof. Certainly being able to have fun with each other as a married couple is a good thing, certainly we can have our own lives as the kids will do without our approval. But also, our kids will now be spectators to our lives won't they? A twist of fate isn't it? But also something where they might also see how two "old people" can love and live as if we were like these same kids that we begat so many years ago. Finally and best of all, their time will come one of these years to deal with their own kids' trials and tribulations. There is some justice in the court of life you know, albeit delayed. Life and the passage of time will pass its own judgment on our kid's lives one way or the other, with or without our presence. And that indeed is the natural order of things.

Jeff to Stephanie April 23, 2007

Sweet Spot

You feel you are at the place in your life you wanted to be in. You feel that regardless of the missteps you might have made, and the demands of your kids, that you are in the "sweet spot" now. You state that you are happy since you are with me and married. And you are certain that all of this inspires you to do greater things in your job. Well my dear, I think you are right.

You do seem inspired and excited about your job. You do seem to be getting the attention of decision makers now. All of that is very good and will serve you well. You will get the chance to get a vice principal's job soon.

Yes as life marches on these times do appear, not in a vacuum of course, they are still surrounded by the swirling mass of everyday living requirements, chores, and trying situations like the on-going struggle with Son and his car, and other things too. After a spate of things that did not work out, tried you, or circumstances that kept you in limbo this is a good change for you. I can detect the excitement in your voice when you talk about such things even on days that are not so good.

For me, this is good news. It is good news for both of us obviously. Accomplishing things is always positive. Now there is of course a cautionary tale in all of this. When a Roman general or emperor had a victory parade down the streets of ancient Rome, it is said that a slave or servant whispered in his ear the warning that "all glory is fleeting". So even with this success, keep the trying times in the back of your mind since they usually will return in some form, and don't forget family since it outlasts and transcends a mere job or career. So when the olive branch of a VP job is placed before you, keep the rest of your life in perspective as it provides the support for your success and the ability for you to be victorious in the future struggles that certainly await you.

Jeff To Stephanie April 26, 2007

Giving Your All

Giving your all. You said this morning that you give all that you have at work. That is OK, but what do those people who receive so much from you ever give back to you? It is true that some of the little kids have shown you some real affection and that you do get compliments from your management, but at the same time you seem lately to be a bit worn out. In that sense, because each year brings a new group of kids to give to, perhaps one might pace oneself in the area of giving so much.

Like in what I do, clients can want everything you have. In that world people get used up and burned out on a regular basis. Consultants either learn to "manage expectations" or they get drained like a beer can consumed by a thirsty person on a hot summer day.

Now, to do a good job in any profession one must give a lot, to do otherwise means you do not meet your goals or the requirements of the job. But at some point you only have so much to give. And the group you may be giving to is something that is hardly permanent. Clients come and go in consulting and in your world each year there are new kids who come and go. Outside of these less than fixed groups you have others in your life that hopefully are more permanent. Family is one such group, and they can take everything you have too. But they too are worthy of what you give since hopefully family and marriage transcends jobs or professions that do not last one's whole lifetime.

If you give everything to groups who will not be around or give anything much back to you, what is the point of always draining your emotional reserves for them? They are here today and gone tomorrow with what you have emptied from your own being for their sake. It is true that job demands must be met, but sometimes you just have to say no to an endless list of requirements defined by those who do not hold your interests in their hearts.

The ultimate point is that when one is a giving person, you may have to note how much you are giving and to whom. The people that can and do give you the most back may not be receiving their due from you. And at the cost of wearing yourself out emotionally and sometimes physically. Pacing one's self and measuring what is given to others is a practice that is worth examining in order to be able to give more over the long haul, especially to those who will remain in your life who themselves will and should give back to you in full measure as the panorama of life ceaselessly changes around you each day and year.

Jeff To Stephanie 5/2/2007

Adult Playtime

Yes, taking a little trip to get a much needed break from everything. The pause that refreshes as they say. Indeed, you and I need that respite. Truly we have had a bunch of things to deal with since we married. And we have gotten to know each other much more than we did before, thus causing a bit of friction between us as you know.

Yes we both are nagging at each other, each in our own way. A sure sign we need to get away and play with each other. Figuratively and literally I might add, in and out of the bed too. Certainly, couples can use a bit of recess from day to day living from time to time I think. It keeps one ready to meet the next buffet of challenges that will get served up to us. And we have not had much of a chance to have recess, seems like we have been in detention hall so to speak with so many family things and the chores of two houses to tend to.

And a change of pace and in our routine restores the fun and excitement that was the nature of our past times with each other as you know. Certainly we have lost some of that in the last month for more than one reason.

Regardless, we both love each other as we have

from nearly the start of our relationship. That keeps us together and makes us willing to compromise for the other and ready try to understand each of our sets of eccentricities and weird personality traits at a deeper level.

Ultimately, our love and our intelligence will keep us happy with each other regardless of the tide of things that will wash over us from time to time. We really do have a good life together my dear, so we must regularly go play on our playground together so we never have to face playing by ourselves like we did before we met each other. So now, I hear the recess bell ringing, calling us to put down our toils, and go play a game with each other in the bright sunshine of our love and life together. And thus regain the innocent sense of wonder about each other that brought us together in the beginning.

Jeff To Stephanie May 3, 2007

May 5th

May 4th, the day before my birthday is today obviously. May 5th is my birthday and also the date of Ron's death years ago. Once you said that since we were together this May 5th would be a new beginning for you. And that May 5th would be happy day not some time of sad remembrance.

I truly hope it is a new start for you in relation to that and for me too in fact. In the past, my kids' mom tended to seem to ruin every birthday I had with one thing or another, my mom & dad even noticed it. Thus, many times I did not look forward to my birthdays. Maybe that is one reason I do not per se make a big deal about them. Similarly, May 5th was a not good day for you. While Ron obviously did not treat you like a real wife in many ways, you loved him since you had known nothing better in your life and he was your kids' father. Thus he provided stability for you at least. When that was removed you were cast adrift and May 5th was a day to forget not to cherish. Little did you know that what that fortune teller lady at the fair said about May 5th had come true.

At this time we are married. And you do get treated like a real wife should be treated. Except when we fuss, but we are working on that and we love each other regardless. In that sense, my birthday, and yours too in November, should be happy times with each other and our extended families. While I do not per se put a lot of emphasis on birthdays my mom and dad always made them fun and special for me and my sister. Thus, my wish is that our birthdays together as husband and wife are special as well. Each one giving happy times that will build memories that we will treasure as we get old with each other.

Therefore, this Saturday I trust we will both put away sad thoughts from our pasts and have a wonderful day together seeing Wicked, picking up more beads from Charles, and cooking something nice for dinner when we return to our home. That way, the good things of May 5th and later your birthday in November, will start to fill a glass fully with the fine wine of good and great events with each other that will overshadow old things "seen darkly" in the broken and cracked glasses of our past separate lives.

Jeff To Stephanie May 4, 2007

Good Weekend

Darling, after fussing so much last week, we have redeemed ourselves and our love by having a wonderful weekend. The ISD banquet, seeing Wicked, the "BBQ Shrimp Deluge", going to church, seeing Charles and doing a good deed for him to return the kindness he has shown to us, and of course a lot of love making (mrrrowwww !!!) all combined to make a memorable weekend with one another. It shows that by concentrating on the good stuff we will be happy. True, around all of this good stuff, we had a couple of tense moments, but what couple does not have those even when times are good?

In short, we have found our way again with each other my Stephanie. When we are mad at each other one might tend to think "all is lost". But not so my sweetie, "all is found" with each other once more. We both remembered the many things that drew us together in the first place didn't we? And we recognized better some of the things that do cause some tension. We will keep adjusting for those things. We must always remember that the facets of our beings that attract greatly outweigh the things that sometimes repel us from each other.

Therefore, the cycle of our relationship goes on, better than it was before. We will both look forward to more good times with each other, like our little "mini-honeymoon" we are about to do. And yes we have a few challenges lurking about us, but who doesn't have such a dichotomy if they have a rich life being lived? I am happy being married to you, and I know you are happy being with me. Who would have thought a year ago that we would be in this wonderful state? Neither of us did. Being there now, we shouldn't begrudge it even for a nanosecond.

Jeff To Stephanie, May 7, 2007

Liking Each Other

Indeed, we DO like each other at the same time that we love each other my Stephanie dear. Truly that is a sign that we will be together when other couples disintegrate and part ways. Even when either, or both, of our "rotten" sides rear their ugly heads from time to time. I like liking you that is for sure.

Why do we like each other? Who knows, I just know it is there. Perhaps it is just the fact that both of us are pretty smart. That is no shocking revelation since we both know this is the way it is. But in the end it is what probably drives our relationship at its core.

Since we are both intelligent we both like many of the same things, we look at life in ways that are similar, and we have views on spiritual and philosophical topics that line up with each other for the most part. Or in ways that the other can at least appreciate and tolerate. Regardless, there are many facets to our being.

We are similar but not totally alike. The differences are both good and bad. Sometimes we grate on each other. But most of the time the differences blend together to complement each other don't they? Like the way I plan things out. You are not oriented that way, but when I do plan things out things go smoothly and we have more time for each other and the things we like to do together or singly. A blending, a pallet of personality colors you might say. Pleasant mixtures of tints, like a pretty sunset, yet no two are alike.

The sunset is a blend of colors, especially when a cloudscape is part of the picture. As the sun changes angles when the day draws to a close, the array of colors also changes. The pinks, the blues, the grays all mutate and vary providing an almost endless set of visages to treat our eyes with. Likewise, the ways we are different, and the ways we alike, provide a variety of experiences that make up our life together. Within that envelope of life, we can truly expect an interesting life together I think. One that is beautiful, one that is sometimes trying, but in the end one that is pleasing like a gorgeous sunset. Something to behold I think, something we can look upon with wonder and also with thankfulness for being so unexpectedly blessed at this stage in our lives.

Jeff to Stephanie May 10, 2007

Our Trip

A trip, a trip, a trip, I am ready to go on our trip!!! Yes, a honeymoon finally, even if it is not that long. It will be fun to get away with you, something we have not done. Certainly we are ready for some fun.

Gosh, I am sounding almost like some Dr. Seuss book aren't I? Well, I am ready to go away with you for our little trip south, very ready indeed. We need to go away and NOT do any chores, NOT worry about one of the houses, NOT worry about our kids, and NOT worry about ANYTHING. Not worrying and doing and instead just playing for once are good for the soul and our marriage of course. Indeed, we have stopped fussing, but this will greatly add to our love for each other, the pause that refreshes as it were.

Yes, drive away, sleep late, make love a lot, each good food, go shopping, do stuff as we see fit, it will all be fun. Such times make all of the chores worth doing don't you know. All work and no play make Jeff & Stephanie dull grownups.

Indeed, going somewhere away from our daily routine will be good. We will have to strive to do this from time to time. And one day we must go away for a real vacation to someplace nice. Hawaii, Santa Fe, or Yellowstone, any of the many places we have talked about. Any of them would be wonderful to go to with you my wonderful wife. I do love you so much. I really do. Here or out there some place on a trip to somewhere, or nowhere in particular; any place is good as long as you are there.

Jeff To Stephanie, May 16, 2007

You Said You Had A Fear Of Being Left

You said you have a fear of being left, due to the Papa Charlie et al literally dropping you off at ACU, death, and other things you experienced during your life. I can understand why such things weigh on you my dear, the few times you had some sort of stability it ended abruptly. Now in the present time with the old house issue you have a fear in the back of your mind, driven by those events that left you empty and not cared for, that I might leave you if something bad happened in reference to that.

Well, not to worry my Stephanie dear. That won't happen ever, at least until I die of course. Being married to someone means you do stick by them "for better or worse" you know. It does if you really love the other person. And I really do love you. So I am not going away. And I will not forsake you. Life provides a variety of ups and downs, which will always be true. People who are not true blue are the ones that might wilt like a flower in the hottest sun on a summer day, but not me. I have a bit more fortitude than that. Besides being loyal to you as your husband, might I not need your support one day when something befalls me personally? The assurance that your spouse will be by your side is one hallmark of a good marriage. We have that as part of our relationship my Stephanie. Always remember that.

Both of us have been through trying times before my love. And both of us have survived such trials, and have been made better persons as a result. Even bad times can bring good times when they are past. The night becomes day as it were, or there is no sunshine without the rain as you have said many times. Thus, one must always keep this cyclic nature of life in mind as you live day to day. You have to remember that difficult times seldom remain present forever so that you can continue to live each day and not be troubled unduly.

Remember this quote I have told you about before, and maybe written to you about as well? *"**Perhaps all the dragons of our lives are princesses who are only waiting to see us once beautiful and brave**"*. In other words, even something bad may have something good within it, or around it. At least that is what I think the poet Maria Rainier Rilke meant. And lo and behold, you were asked to interview for the vice principal's job today. Right before your eyes now there are things that are both good and bad swirling about. Perhaps the poet was on the right track.

Therefore, one can look forward to better times

ahead even though the present may also bring doubt and uncertainty. Together we have a good life, even though rotten things happen that beset us. And together we always have our love which binds us and brings us happiness. Truly that will conquer any force that may try to bring unhappiness to us and we too will become "***beautiful and brave***" for the rest of our years.

Jeff To Stephanie May 21, 2007

Your Most Recent Interview

Some thoughts on your latest interview. Well, another lesson in group dynamics, or lemming-like behavior in human beings. Well, lemming-like may be too strong of an adjective to use but certainly there seems to be a pattern in how they interview people as you do point out. It does seem like they pre-select who will get the job but due to appearances and procedure they do interview other people who are also qualified for the job in question. In the end, they will most likely pick their political favorite. Such behavior is par for the course in groups that perhaps might be somewhat provincial or in-bred in a sense. And that is something you can't do anything about.

Of course, all of this frustrates you a bit. It would frustrate me too. But you either have to work in the system or find another one to work in. Regardless, I stand by you. But the point ultimately is that you are a very capable woman, you know a lot, and you do deliver what is asked of you and much more. Without playing politics or kissing the disgusting nether regions of people you work with.

So my love, I have confidence in you and hope and trust you get the position you want. In spite of the seemingly endless waves of people who seem to be bent on placing their cronies in such positions. But that is the nature of groups of people isn't it? That is just a part of life that we have to deal with in and around the happy times we create in our own little world, on our own without some political group burden, at our comfortable house with a swimming pool near the pretty park we enjoy and live close to each day of our married life together.

Jeff To Stephanie May 24, 2007

Dreams

Well, you had some vivid dreams you have told me about. And last night I had one. In it, something had happened to you, you were dead and gone. I felt lost and of course very upset and sad. My mom and sister were in the dream, trying to comfort me. But that did not help, all I wanted was to get you back. In the dream I went outside. In my hand I was holding what appeared to be a small cereal box. On its back was a photograph of you. Your hair was a bit different, shorter and a bit curly, but it was you with your big pretty eyes, maybe looking a bit younger like you do in some of the pictures in the box out in the garage. I kept looking at it knowing you were not there.

Then somewhere away from my mom and sister I looked up to the sky streaked with cirrus clouds and kept crying out in tears "Stephanie, Stephanie, Stephanie". "Please talk to me Stephanie". "Why are you gone?" Of course you never answered back from The Great Beyond. I cried out to no avail, death being final and without a return. I just kept looking at the picture of you on the box, feeling my world was gone.

Truly, emptiness filled my mind and heart in that alternate, conjectural world, one unfamiliar but yet still recognizable even though totally unreal. Thankfully I woke up, this was about 1:30 AM, and went into the kitchen and got a drink of juice and shed a couple of little tears.

The dream really shook me up my dear; it was hard to get that picture of you from the dream out of my mind. But I went back to sleep and awoke with the alarm of course to find you still by my side safe and sound as you had been all night in our cozy bed that is usually used for sleeping curled up with each other and making passionate love.

Now what does this dark visage from Dreamland mean? Who knows, maybe my subconscious mind was reacting to the combination of the latest turmoil with my kids and to us loving each other more than we ever did after our recent trip down south. Things being good with each other, does my inner self fear that I might lose you? You even asked recently if I ever got a feeling something bad was about to happen. Regardless of what mental currents made this flow forth from the sea of my deepest ego or id, it makes me realize even more that we should *always enjoy* each other and find *great joy* in the little things we see about each other. Every day we are together should be a *celebration* of what we have with each other my love of all loves. Even amongst the sharp thorns that that the darker rose bushes of life may shoot up into the quiet garden we tend together in marriage. Indeed, we have finally gotten it right haven't we? We should treasure this fact without hesitation, and enjoy the coming years we will have with one another.

Jeff To Stephanie May 25, 2007

Cabals And Clicks

Cabals and clicks: groups of people without enough productive tasks to occupy their small, pathetically inept minds. Unfortunately you are beset by one such group right now at the other school. These "groupies" as I sometimes call them seem to view you as a threat, projecting their inner disdain of their own manifest and pervasive inadequacies, onto you to create angst in your life.

It does make one angry to have to waste one's productive time defending one's self against their insidious and mindless assaults. These attacks are the work of people who are less than honorable and also less than competent. Why else would they waste time doing such things? The more they make others look bad, the less other people might look at them and discover their many short-comings.

It seems most groups of people are populated by such human lemmings. We have seen that recently of course with Commode…err….Code Blue. Mindless ninnies who wanted to cast doubt on our relationship when they knew nothing about it. They themselves in some cases were unhappy in their own worlds and thus felt no one else could possibly possess a happy existence. Surely such thoughts are those conceptualized by self centered morons. And endless waves of such dolts seem to batter our shores on a regular basis right?

Without sounding like some broken record, surely such actions are a cautionary tale teaching us to keep our distance from people in many cases, and of course to defend ourselves against the vicious psychotic blitzkriegs that they launch seemingly from nowhere against our ramparts guarded only by ourselves and our morals and upright actions. So my love, we must always tighten our helmet straps and prepare for the worst but always hope for the best. Such is the fabric of life in a universe populated by people who are even more imperfect than we are.

Jeff To Stephanie June 1, 2007

The Ebb And Flow Of Life

The ebb and flow of life. Life, like the ocean's tides, rises and falls around us doesn't it my dearest? Like the ongoing messes with our bunch of kids. One set of children calms down while the other set of offspring presents us with a new set of issues.

This rise and fall of waters that is sometimes rough pulls at our heart strings and tugs at our very being. If we did not feel these things we would not care for our common brood. But we do feel these things and thus we know we love our kids and feel for them, especially when some of them are hurting due to worrisome and negative forces besieging them that are outside of our household and our direct control. And are certainly not within their power to directly influence in some cases either.

I guess this seemingly constant series of ups and downs is just the nature of life at this stage of our existence perhaps. We see events that certainly indicate our kids are growing up, but also events that indicate that they still have more lessons to learn and choices that they must eventually make so that their adult lives will be good.

The difficulty with this situation is that we, in different degrees, want to solve their problems and be done with the difficulties. But therein lays the dilemma. We can't solve their problems ultimately. They as adults, or young adults, still have the responsibility to make their own decisions and choose their own path, wherever that leads them for better or worse. We can only watch and facilitate at this juncture. We can't do everything for them like we could when they were little. Even though with hearts that ache for them, and sometimes eyes shrouded by tears for their hardships, and even agonies, we can really do so little for them.

Knowing that and watching them succeed or fail is hard since we love them. But sitting in our spectator's seats while they are out on the field playing the game of life is what we must do. They have to make the calls and execute the plays in order for them to grow up into good and responsible adults. We can't do that for them. If one still tries to do that it will also make it hard to enjoy our own game and its plays. While we love our kids and will help them, we have to live our life too. We can't live their lives for them. Remember, there is nothing wrong with enjoying what we have with each other; we have the right to be with each other, and happily love, and joyously live our own lives as we get older together. Our four kids will hopefully realize these truths as they mature and they themselves one day get to the same stage of life as we now find ourselves in. Thus, life will also ebb and flow for them too. The tides of their own life oceans will find their way as it has ultimately with ours.

Jeff To Stephanie June 1, 2007

Our Kids, Our Kids

Our kids, our kids, our kids. Just in this week so far we have some adventures with them right? From the 5:30AM call from Son about your daughter to my daughter's pleasant visit we have experienced an array of things have we not? Such swings of things are par for the course aren't they? Or is it fate or just chance? Who knows, it is what it is. Such things will transpire at this stage in our lives as our kids grow up. Certainly we should be prepared for more of such things I would say.

It just goes to show that we are spectators as we have discussed many times. And it shows that as time goes on, things will many times straighten themselves out. Or turn the other way too. Or still seethe in the background. In the end, with four kids becoming young adults, there will be many things that will surprise us over the next several years. Some will please us, some will try us, and some will no doubt sadden us too. As we think back about our own lives, certainly we caused the same reactions ourselves. Such stuff is the nature of maturing I say.

So what do we do in reaction to these things? As I said we are mostly spectators, we can't do much even if we wanted to about how our kids live their lives. Nor should we really. They are adults now, well most of them anyway, but regardless they are free to choose how to live their lives and proceed with their existences without our approval or supervision. Of course, they should accord us the same thing. God forbid, their parents can have lives and love too? Surely not they might say. Surely we can live our life too I say my dear. We can still care for our kids and at the same time love them, help them, and be good to them.

Certainly, this is not a contradiction. Certainly, this is how it should be as our nest is emptied and our little birds fly off to who knows where on their own. What is not certain is where our nestlings will themselves build their own nests. What tree, or in what forest, they will someday land on is unknown. Over time they will have to visit our little nest and let us know won't they? Maybe bringing their own little noisy hatchlings to see us two old birds as our feathers get grayer.

Jeff To Stephanie June 6, 2007

Having Fun With Each Other

Having fun with each other. This morning you said how much fun it was to go walking after supper and then getting in the pool to relax and talk to each other. Getting in the pool last night at 1AM on a work night to cool off was fun too. Certainly that was something we will probably remember our whole lives since it was so odd and so spontaneous. Such things show me that we do have a lot of fun with each other my dear. Indeed, both of us are different from most people and that is one of the biggest reasons we like to spend time with each other, regardless if it is play time or chore time. Or morning time, or daytime, or at 1AM. The point is that we do really like each other and very much enjoy doing things together.

Such a commonality of activities should bring us happiness across the years to come. Couples that are close and do stuff together do seem to stay together happily. Being in a vacuum or going off all of the time to "do your own thing" does not seem to be conducive to really being a couple. Many couples nowadays seem to be married but are not really together.

The "me generation", which we are part of, carries its quest for self identity to an extreme sometimes.

It seems they will likely miss out on the fulfillment of being close to someone in all areas of life by seeking solo activities that may provide short term pleasure, but no long term safety or true satisfaction. This is not to say one can't have their own interests or hobbies or opinions. We certainly have those things, but they do not preclude melding together as one in many areas of our lives.

I think many people in this age forget that they will get more out of life by giving to, and joining with, someone who is their mate than they will get if they simply go their own way all of the time.

So, we do have our playtime with each other just about every day we live. I think it is a good thing. Why else did we marry? Just to simply co-exist? Nope, while we did not need each other emotionally or financially, we wanted each other. And from want comes the desire to be with each other no matter what is going on in our lives. Surely, this is what most couples want to have isn't it? Shouldn't it be what they want if that is missing in their lives? Looking around us I am not so sure what others want or what they have, but I am glad I have you and all of the time we spend with each other. I'll pass on having a life alone that is but a futile emotional soliloquy filled with emptiness. I will enjoy the rest of our lives together being out for recess on our own little playground of love as we attend the school of life together as classmates.

Jeff To Stephanie June 13, 2007

Dreading A Holiday Family Get Together

Dreading a holiday and family get together. Father's Day draws nigh, and I dread it somewhat. We are going to at least meet my daughter on Sunday, but maybe not my son due to his anger at me driven by his vague conceptualization that I should "listen to him more", or should we say tell him what he wants to hear and not describe reality to him.

Yes reality rearing its ugly head once more to another one of our four kiddos. A familiar theme for us isn't it my dearest? Another kid not wanting us to draw a picture rooted in what is really happening as opposed to something that to me seems to be outright fantasy. Such as my son's descriptions of how adult relationships should be or will be when he has one. Outright poppycock I say his words are. Those ideas have no basis in what is a good and normal existence obviously. They present a dark prospect for his life if you ask me.

And as we both know there is nothing concrete either of us can suggest to him as a solution to his plight that he will at least entertain in his mind. Such a quandary is hard to deal with even though

I myself remain calm about things in general. One hurts for him but at the same time one must go about daily life since there is no direct way, per se, to help him get out of the tar pit that he now immerses himself in. Thanks in great part to other forces whose emotional gravity pulls him towards a singularity of woe each day. Well, we won't go into detail about what fearful black holes lurk in that part of his universe will we? I just hope he never drifts across the deadly event horizons of such dark collapsars and his life is destroyed like atoms being torn into particles so elementary that they are no longer matter as we know it by such unimaginable and titanic gravatic forces.

So what does one do on Father's Day when one of those I fathered is gripped in a maelstrom of angst and anger towards me and you as well? I hate to say it but steer the course even though it will be hard for us and harder still for him. Someone has to be realistic with him, even though that path is fraught with hardship yet to come, and on a scale that is not clearly seen but yet already dreaded by us all. Dreaded in part even by some of those spinning black holes who themselves who are not really dark lords of some dreadful existence. As such, even we have to deal with that aspect of this dilemma too don't we? We are surrounded by panoply of forces that do not yet work to the same goal we want to strive for. And thus also contributes to the feeling of dread for a day that should be one of love and happiness alone for me and one young man I fathered many years ago who ***is*** capable of being in the light of happiness and love that we find ourselves surrounded by each day. If he would only steer past the dark nebulas in the otherwise bright blue and white spiral arms of his own life's galaxy. If only he would not be drawn into the darkness of a figurative black hole and torn asunder as he seems to now be. Regardless, he will have to astrogate himself to a safe, warm yellow star like the figurative sun of our own life together.

Jeff To Stephanie June 14, 2007

One Year Ago We Met

Now my love, do you recognize this flower arrangement? I bet you do since it is an image of the little bouquet I sent to you at Kimmel to celebrate the fact that we have known each other a whole year. A small bouquet but the anniversary of a big event in our lives.

And what has this year brought to us? Meeting each other in CERT class, then liking each other, then loving each other, then marrying each other, and of course now nearly eight months of marriage and all of the events we have seen with one another. I certainly consider this passage of time to be quite important. A WHOLE year of our lives, a WHOLE year of our lives spent together. It is hard to believe that fact in a sense. But not really, it is reality for us both obviously. A good reality, and not some nightmare or a figurative prison sentence you know. But some little bit of paradise, or heaven found, on this small part of Earth that we call our home in Fort Worth. Even when we fuss it is a good thing to be with you Stephanie. It is ***very*** good to be with you and I truly at this point in time have a hard time imagining not being with you.

So three little orange roses I had Kelly's Florist

send to you at Kimmel where you are teaching summer school, which is not far from your beloved Mowder of course. Three for ***"I always loved you, I love you now, and I will always love you"***. I know you will enjoy those bright and shiny blooms, small flowers to symbolize our rather large love for each other. Just as I have enjoyed sending them to you this Thursday which is more or less one year to the day last year that we first laid eyes upon each other.

Little did we know that day what our lives would be like one year later did we? And I look forward to our next annual recognition exercise, the first anniversary of being married whereupon we shall renew our vows with one another, hopefully surrounded by our extended family. Some of whom were obviously a bit surprised at what we did last Halloween at the Unity Church. Hopefully, in the end they will not be surprised to see us happy and still in love then and also over the years to come.

Jeff To Stephanie, June 21, 2007

Once More Into The Breach Dear Friends

"Once more into the breach dear friends". Yes a line from Henry V if I remember right but it certainly catches the spirit of us toiling in the mud and rain to fix the drainage problems in the yard caused by the continuing ***Diluvium*** doesn't it? It shows that you and I do usually work well together on projects in and around our houses. And why not I say? You and I are both hard workers and do know a lot. But especially since we are a lot alike in some areas and of course deeply love each other, even amongst sometimes fussing.

And yes we do love each other; I certainly will marry you again come 10/31/2007 as you say you will to me. Indeed, I would be more than happy to marry you time and time again over the coming years. Yes I do love you a lot Stephanie, I really do. As I know you really love me.

And our love keeps us straight when life throws us curves, like those pitched from our kids. The buffet of worries and issues never seems to get smaller does it? The items on that menu just seem to change never lessen. I guess that is just life when a couple has four kids becoming grownups. Yes, only one is really a kid based on age but in their hearts and minds they are not yet fully grown.

And therein lays the challenge, the struggle, and the battle The Bard refers to in a way. In Henry V, "into the breach" refers to a battle in a war if I remember right. Well, some of these issues with the kids are certainly a struggle aren't they? And since we are their parents and love them we are thrust into the breach of that figurative war in some ways. Each of our kids wants something unique to their own psyches, and we have to respond in some way to those needs and wants. Sometimes the response is of course "NO", but you get the picture, we are regularly canvassed at the very least to do something.

Well, as floods and kid's issues swirl around us, I know I love you deeply, like your company, and enjoy being with you. Truly, the thought of being alone and single again is not something I wish to entertain at all. Being married to you is a very good and fulfilling thing. I agree with you that to have NOT married would have been idiocy. Surely, our love will strengthen us as we fight in the breach, and keep us from being defeated by the woes that pop up out of the ground like ugly weeds in our otherwise warm sea of grass that represents our life together.

Jeff to Stephanie July 9, 2007

Personalities

I do love you my dearest Stephanie. Even with some of things in your personality that drive me to near insanity on occasion. Well, not really that far my dear, but like all couples we both irk each other some. But you know, the things that bug me about you relate to the fact they are in areas where we are opposite. Like me being regimented and into planning and you being impulsive. These are things that are basic to our beings. Thus, when they appear they perhaps cause more emotional angst than they otherwise would. Thus, when something happens in such an area, it does cause a few sparks.

Well, we know that we are alike but yet different. Regardless of the areas of difference, we are more alike than we are different. And the areas of personality convergence are in the areas of life that we hold to be important: being faithful, working hard, doing the right thing, loving our kids & families, and things we enjoy doing for fun. To us, those are the values and habits that are at our cores and also make a person good, happy, and productive. Those are the most important things to us in life in short. Therefore, these other parts of our personalities are not so important in day to day life are they?

Well, these other areas can be important too since they still relate to the persons we are at a basic level. So we have to be mindful of how those things are perceived by each other. And sometimes adjust some of our behaviors for each other. And at the same time know that we both love each other without hesitation. In the end, this love is what keeps us patient with each other as we still get to know each other more deeply, even after being together a whole year.

So all in all, I know we are happy being married to each other. Both us know we cannot imagine not being together. Truly, if we had not married or delayed our wedding we would have been unwise. It is natural for us to be a couple, and that is how we shall stay to the end of our lives. Joined at the hip even though when some differences arise we may want to squirm away from each other, the ties that bind us together as one remain strong and alive as they were in the early days of our romance when our love blossomed and bloomed so large and bright.

Jeff to Stephanie July 12, 2007

Almost Married One Year

Yes dearest, we are about to be married for an entire year. And what a busy year it has been. We have, and still are, blending our two households, dealing with our brood of kids and their growing up trials and tribulations, and of course getting to know each other better each day. Yes indeed we HAVE been busy. And it seems the "to do" list is not getting any shorter. But that is OK I guess, I think most people do not have lives that are without events and tasks.

But back on being married for a year my love. Looking back over the time since we met, our lives are very different than they were. Certainly that is a statement of the obvious, how could our lives be the same after being wed? They couldn't, they had to change. It has become something new for us, and for our families too even though in some cases they show angst or other emotions that to us are alien given the fact that we are together due to our love for each other. If two people receive ill-will due to a positive thing like true love, what on earth would they get if their reason for being together were less than good or usurious? I don't want to know actually, our lives as they are seem to be complicated enough some days. In the end, life did mutate into another organism, a different species of existence regardless of what form others outside of our orb thought we would, or should, possess.

And this pattern of change will continue. As we are together our lives will change more over the years, much of the time due to people outside of our doors and events outside of our control. But also due to how we keep learning to understand each other and live with each other. Even when we have fussed, we have learned something positive as a result. And when we don't fuss we certainly also gain knowledge about the other as well.

So more years will pass being together my Stephanie dear; I look forward to them even though we will be getting old for sure. That is OK too, we will enjoy each other's company as we enter into the twilight of our own lives even as our four kids enter into the prime of their own. This is the natural order of things; this is how it should be. We will move across the horizon of our own distant wedding anniversaries yet to come and unseen over time, one after another each year we are one. And we will be changed by our travels through life together. Changed into something better, and greater, than what we are now.

Jeff To Stephanie July 17, 2007

What Will Our Families Think?

And what will our families think about us renewing our wedding vows? My mom asked why we were doing that. My sister had no negative comment. Who knows what my kids or yours think of the idea? Will all of them really be happy that we, God forbid, are happy and wish to do this? Or will they think it is silly? Or will they simply show up and say or think nothing one way or the other? Or even feel uncomfortable in some way that we cannot know? I have no idea right now; surely one could expect a buffet of emotional dishes to be served up during the event, even though such things may be kept from us out of being polite.

As you have asked before, why aren't they happy for us? Well, I think they mostly are happy for us now. Either they have gotten used to us being together or they really like the fact we are a couple. I hope it is the latter but still I have my doubts about what some of our family really thinks I think you would agree. And as we have remarked to one another, they will expect us to agree with their choices for mates or relationships without any dissent being tolerated.

One way or the other we are a couple and will be until one of us dies, and afterwards even since the ties of family live on after its members pass on. They will need to get used to the idea of Jeff and Stephanie Turner as a couple, won't they? Not Jeff Turner and Stephanie Long as it were before we wed. That era of our lives is gone forever. And good riddance to being single I say, being married is so much more satisfying in so many ways. And I should be a good thing to be married, and it is with us.

And therein lays the ultimate reason why they should be glad we are renewing our wedding vows, reenacting our marriage ceremony as it were. That we are happy together should raise their spirits not dismay them. Wouldn't they want us to be happy for them if the roles were reversed? Maybe as they see us enjoying each other perhaps they will learn from our unintended example, that two people can be happy and love each other in spite of life's problems and issues and our own personalities. That perhaps they could learn how to be happy with someone, knowing full well that no couple is a perfect match ever and that no one is perfect and without past mistakes, and also rejoice at our happiness.

And one day apply those lessons to their lives, by finding a good mate and a good relationship that we also could enjoy and be happy to see.

Hopefully one day some of our kids will invite us to see their vows re-lived, and remember that in a way we taught them to do that purely out of our love for each other.

Jeff To Stephanie July 17, 2007

Do You Remember These Pictures?

Do you recognize these pictures my Stephanie? You should since I have used them before on previous notes to you. But they come again into my mind since they make me feel a certain way. To me they convey a sense of timelessness and a visage of something undefined but yet calm that goes on forever to an always receding horizon. A place I wish we were at when the "to do list" of our life gets too large. In such times as these when we feel a bit compressed, I wish we in the "wide open spaces" that these art prints show.

In them, do you notice there are no people and very few things visible? They perhaps convey a view of a simpler life. In this modern age, it seems few people have lives that are straight forward or not chaotic. Unlike what we may think of ourselves we maybe are not so different from the people I call "human lemmings" who seem to rush blindly about very fast to ***nowhere*** in particular, thinking that they will be happy or content merely by "doing something" all of the time. Such people might think that places shown in these pictures are ***nowhere***. But I do not think that as you know.

I however think the places that are filled with emptiness and solitude ***are somewhere***. Somewhere one can clear one's mind and refocus on what is important, if only figuratively since we are *here* not out *there*. Even if we can only transport ourselves to these places in our mind's eye they can still change our mood and our viewpoint by knowing that life is not necessarily made better by always being busy. But instead it is made better by doing the right things and making time for yourself and those you love dearly. And by doing so, we make where we are now better even though the locale where we live is far from empty and is filled with the hustle and bustle of urban life.

So yes my love, I do wish you and I were out somewhere far from the pavement, traffic, and the endless tidal wave of chores, familial tribulations, and the like. It is also true that as responsible people we can never run away from such things, or forsake our children or other family members, but it would be nice to simply disappear for a while and just be together under an endless sky surrounded by nothing in particular except the wind and the silence in a place illuminated by the bright sun and shrouded by an occasional cloud above our heads. And therefore be renewed by the calm that such an expanse would give us.

Jeff To Stephanie July 18, 2007

Angst And Worry

My dear, I was very glad and touched that you called this morning sensing my concern about your mood last night. You feel that you caused worry and angst in my life due to the feelings of my son mostly. Well my love, as I said those feelings of his would be there regardless, if I was single and without you, if I was with someone else, or under most any set of circumstances. If you really look at the state of things, isn't it everyone else that is filled with angst? I'm not the one getting upset at everyone else and what they do if you recall. You are letting them fill you with worry my dearest even though you now have been given what you wanted for so long in your life. Someone that loves you in all of the ways a wife should be loved.

Simply put, the shortcomings of others are driving you into worry. But remember you cannot change what they do. You cannot change what they think. You can control only what you do, and of course greatly influence what I do since we are together. Truly, there are enough things on our plate without one heaping a new helping of to-dos or worries onto the already large and high pile of things we need to address on many the fronts of our joint existence. As I said in our talk this AM, one still has to live one's life, one still has to enjoy that life, without regard to the things one cannot control like the perceptions of kids or parents. You know, the old saying "you can't please everyone" applies here does it not?

No matter what you do, not everyone will agree with or bless your thoughts or course of action. If that is the case, why worry about it? If you try to please everyone and try to fix things you cannot change, you will wear yourself out ultimately. You will have no energy left for the one or ones that are closest to you. That is, one can exhaust one's self with worry about things that are unchangeable and have nothing left for the things you can have some influence over.

Even so, that does not mean one will be irresponsible or uncaring. Far from it, one must do what is right, but tempered with the knowledge that there is only so much one can really do. And only so much one can do effectively. Mere activity is not a sign of how effective you are, one can always be "going nowhere fast". Therefore, you have to prioritize your to do list and try to choose what battles you fight and when. And continue to enjoy life from day to day. Otherwise one can be consumed by the heat of a blaze whose fire is literally unquenchable, like a moth that got too close to the fire as they say.

So my love, we must address the things we must deal with. But at the same time we must always remember to nurture our relationship which will over time transcend these things. If so, our love will remain constant and strong as the panoply of life's challenges change around us.

Jeff to Stephanie July 30, 2007

New Beginnings

New beginnings. Well my love as summer is winding down (hopefully towards the coolness of the fall) we find ourselves beginning some new things in our lives. My new project, a somewhat changed workplace for you and the usual swirl of our kid's ever changing lives and activities. As you know things always change, and they keep doing so. Nothing much stays the same for very long does it in life?

And we are not staying the same either. We are closer now than we were when we got married nearly a year ago. Yes, we sometimes still frustrate one another but our love keeps on going in the direction of being more certain and more comfortable. Truly we are happy with each other and we know we are much better off as persons being a couple. And of course we shall re-emphasize this fact soon when we renew our vows and get married "again". This too is a beginning of sorts, the official beginning of our second year as a married couple. This is a good thing I say.

Outside of our love remaining strong, while changing to be even more firm, our relationship is an island of stability in the sea of ever changing life you know. As new roads in life's journey are unveiled we can look back in our rear-view mirror and see ourselves together as we have been for over a year now. Seeing that fact we can safely go down the new and sometimes rough roads of existence knowing that each other is a safe haven smoothing out the many bumps in this road we call life, providing safety and rest when we are tired and beset by troubles.

So my dearest and most "deluxe" wife, I am ready to start new things with you, regardless of what they are, knowing you are by my side and truly love me. I will be by your side, and always love you too with all of my "rotten" heart. Together we will experience many new things as one, and happily so.

Jeff To Stephanie, August 15, 2007

My Dear Competent Wife

My dear competent and industrious wife, I trust that when you read this you will know you have been successful in your big presentation. I know you are very comfortable with the topic and the material. And I know that you can handle the crowd. So I feel you are destined to be successful today, hopefully with people from administration watching you.

Such events are milestones in one's career sometimes. After they have passed into the sometimes foggy realm of one's memories, I hope we will be able to look back and note that your talk today is what made some decision maker really notice what you could do for the whole school district. When you look the part and act the part, one usually gets the chance to take a new step up the career ladder you know. Surely this will be the case with you, especially since you know your stuff and look like a principal in your beige suit outfit.

And surely you will get the chance to become a principal of some type someday soon. I feel you will get this chance, but I am not sure when given some of the dynamics you describe as being present there in the district. If you have to pay your dues by doing these presentations and other things like summer school, so be it. I do not see such additional duties and responsibilities as being bad since they each give you a chance to shine in front of your management. Looking good to the bosses never hurts does it?

Now for the near term we will need to celebrate your talk today. You can't work all of the time, you have to treat yourself some when you are successful in order to be able to keep up the pace to ensure further triumphs. So we will have to have some fun this weekend, maybe in the sun in our pool, or getting Hatch green chiles with which to make a fine meal, and of course something romantic in our cozy, little bedroom too. Such little things are also successes and triumphs as well. They show the success of our love and our marriage, the happiness from which peps us up and gives us the energy and urge to do well in our work lives.

Jeff To Stephanie August 16, 2007

Selling Yourself

Selling yourself whilst swimming in a seemingly endless sea of idiots. That is how it seems to me my dear. You know what you are doing and you are smart. And have all of the required certifications. But yet you are stymied by the politics of the good-old-girl, not boy, network at the ISD. Twice you have applied for higher level roles and twice the insider's fem-buddies were chosen over you. Well, that is how many groups work as you know and is not a surprise. Honestly it is not an evil thing either while it frustrates you greatly. It is simply human interaction in groups at work. It merely shows that you should sell yourself more in order to become "one of the girls" so to speak since this ISD is a matriarchy overall. While you sold real estate in past years, you seem to be somewhat reluctant to sell your skills in the present age for some reason. You seem a bit timid in this regard.

I think that your hesitation to push the higher ups in your favor is due to at least a couple of factors. One reason is that you, like me, are hesitant to publicly show how smart and capable you are. If you get hit with arrows by people that are worse shots than you sometimes one is reluctant to draw the bow string back and fire off another arrow towards a target. Another reason is that you simply are honest and not a "schmoozer', you do the right thing based on merit or morals and you have a hard time understanding those who do not operate this way. I am like that too some. But I do see the inherent self interest, sloth, incompetence, and downright evil in people much easier than you do.

I think your childhood makes you reluctant to see the bad side of people and things since you saw so much that was not ideal or story-book like. Thus, you recoil when faced with the ugly realities of how people act, especially when it is in a way that is not favorable to you and your interests which are of course always benign and beneficial to those around you.

So what do you do to increase the odds that your desires are given favor by the educational oligarchy? Very simply you have to sell yourself. Not in a way that matches the endless waves of self centered morons that sometimes seem to beset you, but of course in a positive way that shows what you can do and how you can benefit the ISD. You simply have to put your feet forward more than you have done before to get in front of Those Who Lead. You have the skills and the knowledge my dear, you just need to be more direct and get face to face with the people that ultimately will decide on how far you will move up the school food chain. Therein lays the challenge for you I think. In a way, you need to apply some of the skills you used in real estate to make you career case. You are the product, not some house of course, but you still have to sell YOU, which is an intangible and intellectual offering, to buyers who are reluctant to make the "purchase" since they do not know you well enough. That is, you are not "one of the girls", at least not yet.

But by getting in front of these figurative buyers more frequently, like you did last week, you can ultimately get their name on the contract so to speak my dear. You just have to put your sales hat on so to speak and regularly find ways to talk to the people over you so they will know what you can do. By using that modus operandi, you should succeed in time. There is no reason for you to fail.

Jeff To Stephanie August 21, 2007

Victory Against The Looming Threats

Victory against the looming threats of the "Idiocracy". Well, enlisting the help of the new Vice Principal certainly has paid off: victory against the Odd Gaseous One and her deluge of self centered acts not beneficial to you. Perhaps finally some of the people not at your home base now know just what you are made of and what you are capable of. It seems that this may be so at long last.

Indeed, you have endured a lot of slings and arrows from her and some of her moronic fellow travelers there and elsewhere. Surely, your intent on doing the right thing has finally triumphed over their narcissistic mediocrity and outright sloth. Yes, I may be sounding a bit harsh in my descriptions of some of the people that have given you grief, but honestly the adjectives apply unfortunately. This is a shame to be sure and let's hope that their lack of competence does not rub off on the many kids they teach.

But for now, your good intent has been more firmly established and you now have the tools you need to do your job well, which is a good thing since you have the drive and the good heart to try to help your students as much as possible. Maybe now Those Who Lead will see how you can help the wider universe of the schools adorning the educational galaxy that is the school district you are in. Surely you will be a very bright star that will be a beacon to those traveling within it and also to the kids who will one day leave it for hopefully better worlds in the figurative sea of suns that comprise life's broad universe of opportunity.

And you should enjoy this moment, not with some gloating spasm of revenge for the Odd Gaseous One, but instead with a sense of accomplishment and satisfaction with your own talents and abilities. With such internal contentment, you will be able to keep traveling down the long road to getting the position you want within the ISD. There is no reason why you should falter at all my love. With small victories like the one yesterday, you should be able to march on to your ultimate goal and the fulfillment of your dreams that mean so much to you as a teacher.

Jeff To Stephanie August 30, 2007

This Is The Kind Of Place

This is the kind of place I wish we could be my Stephanie when times get tough with various things like have been faced with lately. Wouldn't it be nice to just step out our back door, or front door for that matter, and see nothing but a scene like this? No traffic, no people, no troubles, just something peaceful and quiet like this place.

Looking at such a picture, I really wonder why people like us, and millions others also like us, everyday endure all of the hassles that everyday life throws at us. Society tells us that we have it better than any other generation ever has. In a material sense that of course is true. But is it true in other ways? For example, living in the city as we do we are hemmed in by houses, roads, and shopping centers. Certainly our house is pleasant and quiet, but even the nice park by us is still marked by the presence of our fellow residents. Thus one is never far from someone else, or something. We are always beset by something that takes time, money, or our patience to use or endure. Certainly our ancestors who crossed plains like the one above would marvel at the things we have. But would they be envious of what we have? Or would they make a point to us about the things we have lost? For example they might tell us we have lost ability to obtain the peace that something simple and quiet brings, like the seemingly endless prairie in the picture. So beset by "to dos" and things we forget that simplicity itself brings happiness many times.

Sure, we can drive to such places, but those locales belong to someone so we can't just park ourselves and admire the view can we? While we can briefly enjoy such a peaceful repose, in the end we have to return to the hive that is urban life in the early 21st century. We most surely live longer and have better material things, but perhaps in many ways our lives are not really any better than those of people who lived through the frontier era.

In the past, anyone could go to a place like the one above. And stay if they wanted to. Or move on to another one beyond the wide horizon or over the next range of mountains. Now, we really can't do that. We would have to sell our houses and get new jobs and pay thousands just to move. Back then, having less stuff, someone could do it more easily seems. And get away to some place that offered something new and hopefully better. In that time, one could get a fresh start and in some ways make one's problems go away.

But in end, and coming back to Earth and reality, I know our life is really pretty good my dear, I am not thinking that somehow we could just run away to some unknown frontier and start anew, but sometimes it is nice to imagine being in a place like that empty wide and green expanse with just you, and nothing else, by my side. And have no material things, just our love and our family, to surround ourselves with.

Jeff To Stephanie august 31, 2007

Rainy Days

Rainy days. Today is one of those days. Rain coming up from the south, some of it is heavy and some of it is light. Sort of like our life in general right now. We are burdened, like most people, with a set of things that worry us in varying degrees. These things are of course external to our love relationship as you know. These worrisome things and events, like the showers, come in waves and lines. They wash over us, drenching the lawn of our life together, blotting out the bright sunshine representing the happiness and calm that we certainly wish was always present.

Like the real weather these things wax and wane. One day is more stressful than the next and some times you never know what will happen. Just like the weather. It is full of surprises and unexpected events. But the rain is not always bad you know. Sometimes it has to rain before the sun comes out so the green grass will grow around us. Perhaps we are conditioned to think that life should always be perfect and grand. Like an eternally sunny day. We both know that is not the case, but we certainly wish it were.

Being a weather nut I usually enjoy seeing it rain, and that is true. But I don't like it raining on our happiness however. That is only natural and normal. But like right now when we are worried about some important things seeing the real rain perhaps can bring us some calm and peace while the rain storm that life brings cascades doubt and worry over our together.

However tonight as we assess the state of things, perhaps we can watch the rain and listen to it and find a moment of release from all that worries us right now. Its pitter-patter will remind us that while every day is not always filled with sunshine, in the end even the rain does not last forever. And the sun will shine once more upon our little life together as a happy married couple.

Jeff To Stephanie September 4, 2007

Ahhhhh

Ahhh….perhaps the first cool down of the fall is approaching now. At least that is what the National Weather Service and Chanel 5 are saying right? Regardless, such news and the changes in the sky above us, like the ever modifying angle of the sun, show us that maybe summer is really about to be over.

Fall always gives me more energy and puts a little bit of excitement in my gut. The heat of the summer drags me down you know so the possibility of cooler weather, I assume, just lifts me up. I know it does because I feel this way every year at this time, especially when the first cool fronts finally blow through and give us a hint of what is to come over the next few months as we move towards the even more temperate months of weather. Well, colder more than temperate you know.

Even though when it gets cool we won't be able to go swimming (unless we heat up the pool), that is OK since we won't have to sweat or run the air conditioner. And the air will be clear and the amount of haze and dust will be minimal compared to "high summer" in July or August. A blessing to be sure is delivered with the change to more northerly winds.

And of course, as things get cooler our thoughts also turn to the coming holidays. Turkey Day and Christmas are things we both look forward to. Times for fun and family both, making us appreciate the things, the people that is, that are really most important in our lives, especially each other of course.

And thus our lives will continue, as do the seasons and how they progress one into the other, forever going from warm to hot to cool to cold. And again that way without an end that we can see or understand. And thus we too will cycle through life together, sharing the ups and downs, like the changes in the weather, together. But as I feel excited about fall and cool weather to come so shall we be excited to be together regardless if when bad tidings, like the unpleasant heat of summer, fall upon us. One way or the other the weather will ultimately change for the better as will our lives.

Jeff To Stephanie September 7, 2007

An Unnamed Girl Is Sent Into the Cold

An unnamed girl is sent into the cold, cruel city to sell matches by her equally cold, cruel father. She turns her income over to him and he beats her when he feels she has not sold enough matches. One night the girl, frozen to the bone, lights a match. A glorious Christmas tree appears, bright and blazing. That vision vanishes along with the match when it burns out. The second match she lights shows a splendid holiday feast – a Feast of Illusions. This, too, fades away when the match burns out. The final match she lights reveals her beloved, deceased grandmother. The girl runs to her, never to return to the cold city streets. The next morning, she is found, frozen to death in the street".

My dear, you have been through many things in your life that were not so good. Nothing like what the little match girl you have identified with went through, since you are alive and well, but many tough things nonetheless.

Regardless of your tribulations, you have become a very wonderful person indeed. Your many great and admirable qualities are things I must always keep in mind and recognize above all else about you my Stephanie. Yes, you sometimes irritate me with your somewhat less than organized ways, but that is but a small thing to bear when weighed against your high morals, intelligence, and love for me, our kids & family, and human kind in general. In spite of the woes that befell you at various times past, those things did not make you sad, angry, or sour on life.

It seems that the opposite in fact has happened. You do see the glass half full, more than I do many times, and therefore you are blessed with a good and happy nature and a ***celestial*** light that shows your love of life in spite of its past bad times and the present challenges that confound us. And perhaps I have done the same thing too due to a different set of cards dealt to me by the dealer on existence's poker table. But differently than you since I am such a "black and white" realist who looks on the glass half empty sometimes.

So in a way when we met, we both ran to each other like the little match girl ran to her grand-mother as the last match faded, never again to feel cold and pain but to know only love and comfort without woe or worry. The vast majority of the time our love brings each other in from the cold winds of life to a bright place where we can spend the rest of our lives. Safe, warm, and loved by the other. Surrounded by many good things that bring comfort to our sometimes roughly handled souls.

Jeff To Stephanie October 4, 2007

Kids And Such

Well, we are beset as usual with more kid oriented worries my dear. It does seem like we are being bombarded with a machine gun like hail of figurative bullets each week. And this week and the last weekend has been no different.

And it does wear on us does it not? It makes you prone to worry and it makes me more irritated. Certainly this duality of effects is not good on us or our interactions with one another.

Sounding now like the proverbial broken record, we must always keep in mind that we cannot affect a solution to these situations by ourselves. Much transpires without our knowledge or the possibility of being able to effect how certain events transpire, even though we would like to wave a magic wand of sorts like a good fairy and make everyone's wishes come true like is described in many fables and tales.

But alas, we cannot guarantee that all of our kid's will live happily ever after. It is really beyond our control, and our ability to guarantee any specific outcome for any one of our children. Indeed we love all four of them, and can do some things for them, but in the end they alone have the ultimate power to determine how their little lives will unfold over the coming years and decades. Only they can choose how they will live and what they will accomplish, regardless of what we want them to do or hope they might strive for.

This dichotomy of love for our kids and our inability to ensure a particular outcome for them is the ultimate thing that frustrates us. If only our kids could somehow be inserted into our minds, like in a Star Trek mind meld, and could see and feel what our lifetime of experiences teach us and change how we approach life.

If only they could know what we know derived from decades of hurts, and also victories over adversity, and learn from what we have endured. If only… If only… But that is the point of the situation that we must face, they can't be like us or think like we do since they ultimately are individuals like us.

And they therefore can and will make choices as we did and suffer, or benefit from, the consequences of those actions. Suffice to say, we can largely only watch how their journeys will go as they choose which forks in life's road they travel down. We can't walk with them on the same trail; the way is too narrow for more than one person at a time. So, only after time passes, might we know what destination they will arrive at.

Perhaps only when we are very old and are looking upon the end of our own existence, certainly hoping we lived well and have done well for each other and our now turbulent brood, might we know if they matured into grown ups that somehow mirrored what we are today. And if we are gone when they "wake up and smell the coffee" hopefully they will think back across their own lives, hopefully with the turbulent and difficult things they now face receding into the healing fog of the past, and perhaps silently thank us for what we taught them purely out of our love for them.

Jeff To Stephanie October 10, 2007

Finally

Finally, we have some cooler days now my dear. Indeed fall is a glorious season; we both revel in the relief from the hot days of the seemingly endless summer. The skies are mostly free of haze and dust, the sun's angle bends so that the shadows are longer and the days grow shorter. And the weather overall now changes so that we have northerly winds washing over us sometimes and high clouds streaming above us. All in all, a glorious vista of change, and also one of wondrous beauty for us to behold.

And as these vistas outside change so have our lives changed again. You are now at Mowder, which is something you have hoped for and is a source of relief and satisfaction for you. And for me, the blessed deliverance from driving to Dallas and instead having the short journey to M&M, just a few miles from our house. It shows that more things than just the seasons change you know. Life ever-changing has furnished us a new set of circumstances, this time giving us some pleasant things for a change in opposition the many recent worries about family and our kids which seem to never end.

So we march on down time's long road, not knowing where it will take us, but certainly we can look behind us in the temporal rear view mirror and see where we have come from. Indeed, we can soon look back to getting married a year ago and see the start of our life together. And what a year it has been. And what lies next before us? Only the passage of even more time will show us that of course. Surely, our next year as a couple will have a buffet of experiences served up by life's kitchen, with some dishes sweet and certainly some sour.

But that is the menu all of us get when we go into the dining hall of existence. All we can do is to learn to eat all that is served up to us, regardless if it is palatable or not. And hope that we do not suffer unduly from indigestion, hoping as well to receive some share of satisfaction and delight.

So again we see that fall is upon us, as is another year together my love. The days will dawn one after another until it is winter with some being good and some being bad. But isn't that preferable to not having the seasons of the year and our lives change? I think so. Therefore I will enjoy the seasons of our life together as we pass through them since we are doing so as one with our love as our calendar and also our sure guide. And thus the figurative and real seasons, and years, of our lives will unfold until our time upon this sometimes worrisome orb will end.

Jeff to Stephanie, October 12 2007

The Rain Today

The rain today was certainly a torrent wasn't it my dear? It came in many ways. It poured down on us, it came horizontally at times, and it welled up as run off that made us drive even slower through the low spots on our way to work. Finally it then tapered off and sprinkled itself to an end ultimately.

This cycle of the rain and weather ebbing and flowing is sort of like life isn't it? The types of rains certainly are like different times of our life, either when viewed across the hazy and wide expanse of the long decades prior to now or across the short and many times emotional view of a few busy days. And the lightning and thunder too plays their part. Remember the low growl of the thunder as we left for work this morning? And the bright forks of the many lightning bolts as we went through the intersection at I-35W?

Those events too are like life. The rain one might be compared to the overall stream of events that make up the timeline of our existence. The thunder and its parental bolts, like Thor's Hammer, surely can be compared to the many major events that also sometimes come unexpectedly. The sudden flash illuminating all, the rolling thunder echoing across the landscape afterwards. Likewise are the effects caused by some major or sudden event that is part of our past and its enduring or lasting effect upon us or our families.

As we remember memorable storms and floods like we probably will today's, we also remember many things in our pasts that made impressions upon us. Hopefully we learned from these events, whether or not they were good or bad. And therefore adapted for the better based on the lessons learned from such deluges of life. In the same way we learned from experiences as children that taught us to come in from the rain to avoid getting hit by lightning or getting drenched by a downpour. Staying inside where it was dry to watch and learn from the rain as it passed over us.

So to me, the cycle of a line of thunderstorms is like the line of our lives as seen on the temporal radar screen. It comes and it goes, waxing and waning and giving definition to the day and night, but in the end the rain does ends. As do our lives, which oscillate back and forth in their own rhythm of good and bad until our torrents of love emotion, grief, happiness, hope and fear that make our own storms of individuality pass into the calm of eternity.

Jeff To Stephanie October 15, 2007

Friday And Fun

Well, I always like to start off the day like we did today. By s*****g our brains out after waking up. Truly my dear that is adult play time you know. And what could be better? Nothing that I know of.

Truly, to hold you in my arms and enjoy you, and likewise for you of course, makes one's day in a way that nothing else can. Obviously, we interact by talking and doing many things together, but doing THAT together really makes for one great start to things.

And why shouldn't it be that way? Being in love with each other, more than we were when we married nearly a year ago, means times like that show us that we still love each other with intensity, the intense pleasure is one result of this continued romance and love.

Now tomorrow we have some chores and projects to do like scraping the rest of the wall paper from our kitchen. That surely will be drudgery for me but of course I will help you out a lot so we can get it done. In between scoring and scraping to make way for the western look kitchen, surely we can adjourn to our bedroom to move in a different way. That is, to move rhythmically against each other's bodies to reach a wonderful and intense loving peak with one another. Now that would make me one happy husband and camper. Along with having good booze and food too of course which I will be happy to conjure up for us.

In the end my dear, our love is shown to each other in more than one way isn't it? We do the practical things like create our wills and do the chores. But we also do the emotional and romantic things like love on one another which makes all of the other things even more worthwhile, including the monotony of chores and work. Without that type of thing we would certainly have a cake without icing, which would be dry indeed to the taste. But instead the warm icing of our love is spread on a hot cake fresh out of the oven of our still young marriage for our mutual enjoyment. And thus it will be for us in the coming years as a couple.

Jeff To Stephanie October 19, 2007

And Yet We Now Gather

And yet now we gather under our lives' fluttering banners as they sway back and forth in the brisk winds of life. But what will be revealed with the change in the wind that must yet come to us all? Looking across the years filled with such variations in the atmosphere of existence, we now see ourselves like the very dust that is blown before change's gust front itself. Blown to and from, also like the leaves as they fall from the branches in the gusts as fall draws nearer to the dark of winter, we brace ourselves for the cold breezes and shorter days that surely await us all.

Certainly we can steel ourselves against the harsh and inclement seasons of life, but how much so? Some storms are so severe and violent that even the strongest shelter sways, and sometimes is breached, by the onslaughts of events and the tides of chance. Even the strongest walls can be damaged and thus suffer while staying upright. But the weak surely will falter and yet be rubble in the desolate landscape that many times surrounds even those who persevere against such trials.

And yet how strong can any of us really be? We do not know from time to time how firm our foundation is, or how sound our soul's roofs are.

Can we withstand a hailstorm or vortex of unexpected peril or a flood of uncertain toil or hardship? Only the successive waves of such things passing over time teach us whether or not our fabric is strong enough to bind and protect us from the piercing thorns of a branch violently swayed our way by the forces of life's wind currents.

So once again, the horizon darkens as the skies grey over us and our home. We look with apprehension at the looming walls of woe that never seem to stop their onslaughts against the fortresses of our emotional hearths which are our personal ramparts of strength and resilience. And yet, tried by the fires of these harsh blazes, we try to remain strong for ourselves and those we love, especially when these others, our descendents, are not as strong as we.

They are not yet the wounded and scarred veterans of these lifelong psychic wars. But the time to prove their courage and strength awaits them too on these battlefields, these harsh grounds which give neither mercy nor quarter. As our time in this service has already passed during the long years without leave or relief to provide a panoply of both bitter defeats and yet sweeter victories that ultimately bring meaning to our never ceasing struggles.

Jeff To Stephanie October 25, 2007

Another Year For Us Now Begins

Another year for us now begins, or will on Wednesday depending on how we count the days my dear. Certainly, we could start the new married year from last Saturday when we renewed our vows, and thus married each other again with the good Reverend Roach once more officiating for us. Maybe this year will feature less emotional angst from the family side of our lives; it feels like we have never had much of a break from those trials since we wed 363 days ago. It seems like no one is ever pleased with what we do, yet we never publicly criticize their actions for the most part or question their right to have their own life and choice of existence.

And why is this happening to us? Is it just because we dared to marry and love one another without their permission? I really am not sure. Of course, we have talked about the many currents flowing in this raging emotional river, and it is true that there are many reasons for all of this angst and outright anger. But the causative agents for this series of out of control relationship reactions are still baffling and almost incomprehensible from the standpoint of simple logic and of course the obvious reality of their sources which we both can see. But at some point, I simply have to say enough is enough. I sort of did that Sunday, did I not? Someday soon, this boil has to be burst and the pressure relieved. I do not really want to not have contact with our kin, but sometimes that harsh and simplistic remedy has a certain appeal to me, and to you too as well it seems.

So once more, our special day together was followed by someone in the family laying all blame on our doorstep for their own and other's behavior. And certainly no one asked us how our little occasion went did they? Maybe that says it all. Our behavior, which is pretty innocent, seems to always be questioned while the action of others is accepted without question or query. This constant conflict will most likely have no real end and will be a permanent part of our life I am afraid. If this prediction is correct, our only sure course of action to simply keep our distance in a sense.

We shall offer up our love, communication, and time to be together in fellowship, but at the same time we will not beg for the reciprocation of others. The invitation will be made, but if none accepts it that will be the way it is. We will have to preserve our life together against the feelings of others that are not at all positive to us.

In this rough sea of family tides, we will simply have to make for a safe harbor in each other's arms and in our home. I do not want us to behave like our home is a fortress that only protects us against flights of angry arrows fired upon us, I want it instead to be a place where all of the family is welcome and sees that our life together is a good thing and that our love is true and not a threat to them.

But again, many winds blow against our ship's sails from more than one quarter and it is hard for us to steer clear around the sometimes deadly shoals to calmer waters. But steer clear we must, we have the right to chart our own course as everyone else seems to be doing with the ships of their own lives. Having our own voyage through life is our due, as it is theirs. But we don't have to chart our course with maps and navigation of their sole choosing. Certainly we wish no one else a rough journey, far from it. We want all of our kin, whether they are ours through blood or by our marriage, to also reach a calm sea to sail upon to their own chosen port of call. We simply want to do that too, and thus we two will be together as shipmates on our lifetime cruise to an island paradise of love, to a peaceful beach of belonging to one another under a blue sky free from storms and gales.

Jeff To Stephanie, October 29, 2007

Another Year Begins For Sure

Well my Deluxe Wife, Friend, and Most Wonderful Lover, we have truly started our second year of being married. Of course, with some family issues casting their shadow over us somewhat. But what is so new about that? That has been the story of our little life together from our very first full day of being husband and wife. But none of those events has stopped us from loving on each other and enjoying our new life together. We may not be officially newlyweds any longer but I think we still feel like a pair of them.

Why is that? Because we can still look each other in eyes, like we did this morning, and even with you being very sick and us worrying about our eldest daughter, we can still smile at each other and see that we are happy with other and thankful that we met so unexpectedly. Kind of like people who meet accidentally on movies or TV almost isn't it? In a way yes as we have discussed so many times that neither one of us took the CERT class ever imaginings that we might meet someone, much less marry such a person. I for one am so very glad that we met when we did, started dating, knew we loved each other, and then married to top everything off so to speak.

So here we are on our first wedding anniversary, planning on dressing up like we did at our wedding to be in costume for the trick or treaters that will appear at our home's door. That will be fun, assuming you are feeling better enough tonight to don the wedding dress and veil as you did one year ago. That also shows our playful side with each other, have you ever heard of a couple doing such a thing? I haven't and doubt many couples would think of such a thing.

But we did…and so it is as the Right Reverend Roach states so many times. And so it is with us as a couple: our creativity, our love, our caring all make us a good couple with a good marriage, even with an occasional fuss and all the while enduring the waves of familial angst that batter our shores. And so it will be over the coming years together, we will be happy, have fun with each other, love on each other, and have a good life together, one which we never imagined we would ever have not so long ago. But in the end we find this good thing we call Jeff and Stephanie Turner alive and well and ready for another year as one.

Jeff To Stephanie10-31-2007

A Woman Loved

A woman loved. Yes that is you my Stephanie, you are loved very much be yours truly, your Jeff. And I think it shows on your face, you are happy being loved by someone who appreciates your intelligence and even your quirks like your enjoyment of appliance repairs. Now that is a unique combination for sure, let me tell you.

But again, you are truly loved by me. How else could I write all of these little notes for you when I take a little break from work to clear my head so I can solve some problem? How else indeed? I could not do this if I hated or disliked you. That would be impossible for me to do.

But back on your face of love as shown in the picture. In it you look soft and feminine, not hard and worn at all. Your pretty face simply rounds out the package of wonderful things that makes you up. Your soft and flowing hair, pretty big eyes, and below the picture your deliciously curved figure which I truly enjoy. All in all a very nice package you are my dearest Stephanie.

So indeed you are loved, a beautiful, smart lady who is very easy to look at. Regardless of what you have on at the time…or don't have on at the time honestly. In the end however, it is what is inside of you that makes me love and adore you, enjoy you and want you. And that is worth more than all of the gold in the world to me. Everyday we are together I treasure what I have found in being your husband and the kind, loving person that you are.

Jeff To Stephanie, November 1 2007

A True Thanksgiving Awaits Us

A true Thanksgiving awaits us it seems my dear. And it is about time. After the deluge of fiery familial angst that engulfed our new life together last year it will be a victory of sorts to get everyone in our clan together for some fun and companionship. Hopefully no one will show anger or ill-will that day. Maybe they will all get stuffed with food and some wine they will be too mellow to fuss in any sort of way.

It will be interesting to see how everyone interacts won't it? Your kids and my mom, my sister's bunch and your kids, and whatever other dynamics show themselves during the feast we plan and its sleepy from too much food aftermath. The menu of personalities will be as varied as the menu of food that will appear on the table I predict.

So I hope no one leaves with real or emotional indigestion. I truly want to believe that everyone will get along and maybe even like each other. Perhaps this event longed for is something planted in my being by the relics of the memories of the Thanksgivings I have described to you from my childhood. Maybe those gatherings had tense moments and I was just too young to see or understand what was going on. Even if that is true, the Norman Rockwell like recollections I have of those times are still very vivid in my mind. They are from times I do hold dear and will never forget even though the details of them now fade across the dim view of the decades since then.

Maybe that is how it should be, sometimes we need memories like that to anchor us, to tell us who we are, and where we came from. These views, almost now like dreams, filled by visions of grand-parents, cousins, and other relatives are part of the past but make me feel certain things about the present: a hoped for future that is something like that old era.

While those times are now long gone and many of those people are now dead, buried tens of years ago in a little cemetery seldom now seen, their love, or at least my perception of it, still lingers in my own life even now.

So I am thankful for both the times long ago that were spent with my family celebrating Thanksgiving and also for the fact that we will gather our new, blended clan together as one for the first time this Turkey Day. If we are lucky, our home will be filled with new found familial warmth on a day that is supposed to be very cold. And thus we will paint our own picture of a family together at Thanksgiving that our four children will remember and cherish when they are much older and are thinking back across the long years of their own lives.

Jeff To Stephanie November 19, 2007

My Darling Wife

My darling and loving wife, I was so sorry you were so upset yesterday about the situation with your foster parents. It saddened me to see you so down. I know very well you have been hurt since you were a child by people you loved not returning the love you so freely give. You truly have a large heart and a caring soul, no one could ever say you were evil or without compassion. Certainly, those qualities about you are some of the things that attracted me to you when we met. And they attract me still to you, driving me to be in your loving arms or to hear your calm and reassuring voice.

Now, the sermon Sunday added to the thoughts you were already having about the foster ones, the holiday season reminding you of what you never really had. That is, not really having a real and official family outside of your kids. This has been something that has hurt you most of your life and has also caused sadness for your children. Certainly, this is something that has made your life less good than it could have been, casting a shadow on what otherwise should have been a more bright and happy existence. And at the same time, the good and wise Reverend Roach who married us showed that even these dark events that bring sadness to your heart can also be seen in the light of better things that fill your present life, like our marriage which makes you truly part of a family and not some seasonal guest whose treatment seems more driven by obligation, or guilt even, than by true love and kinship.

These facts and the last message from church reminds me of the words below, which illustrate this situation, words that you know I hold to be dear: ***Perhaps all the dragons in our lives are princesses who are only waiting to see us act, just once, with beauty and courage. Perhaps everything that frightens us is, in its deepest essence, something helpless that wants our love. So you mustn't be frightened if a sadness rises in front of you, larger than any you have ever seen; if an anxiety, like light and cloud-shadows, moves over your hands and over everything you do. You must realize that something is happening to you, that life has not forgotten you, that it holds you in its hand and will not let you fall.***

Yes my dear, you must not let yourself think that life has let you fall. You are in its arms safe now, at least as safe as life can be as the Reverend teaches us, since you ***are*** loved and part of a family.

Our family is not perfect but you are as much a part of it now as me or any of the rest of us, as are your children. Whether it is by blood or by marriage you and your children are one of us now. And perhaps this knowledge will make the dragons of your life cease tormenting your kind soul, showing you what you have now, something you have always wished for. To simply be loved by a family and not cast aside or questioned. Hopefully, knowing that you are really part of a group of kin will keep your emotions from falling downward at this happy time of the year, one which should be centered on family, love, and the remembrance of good times past and loved ones now gone from our eyes but yet still very much alive in the sharp focus of fond memories that should be shared with our children at special times such as now.

In the end your soul should now be landing safely in the open arms of those, especially me, who love you and consider you to be one of their own, never again to fall into hurt from the loss of love or its selfish rejection.

Jeff To Stephanie December 3, 2007

A Bright Aurora

A bright aurora in a dark sky, swirling around a center of the infinite in the sky. A shimmering shape cast against the dark of the night, brining forth illumination where none was seen before.

In some ways my dear you are like that too. You certainly stand out with your intelligence, wide array of talents and your good looks. Certainly you are a rare combination of things, certainly like the always unique shapes and colors of an aurora in the sky, especially one seen in our southern skies. Only once have I seen an aurora for real, one night when I was a little boy. Our neighbor called and he asked me of all people what it was. I told him of course nonchalantly. My mom and dad got a kick out of that let me tell you. The neighbor wondered if it was the end of the world. Nope, just the aurora borealis.

And like that ghostly apparition in the sky that night probably 40 years ago, I have only met someone like you once. Yes, that once is when I met you in our CERT class. Indeed, I was drawn to you and you to me of course. But in the end I knew how unique you were.

Certainly, such celestial sights are something to

behold my Stephanie Celeste. Indeed, your middle name brings forth images of grace and beauty just as the aurora beings such things to a featureless and dark sky. You have brought those things to my life in a special way. Truly meeting you was a once in a lifetime experience, just like seeing that red stream of pale light curving across our northern horizon that night when I was a kid. Only once have I been blessed by such sights, but I appreciate both occasions with my heart and my soul. But especially the sight of your shining self as it illuminates my life by showing me the brighter path to being a better person and being not one so dark, and to loving who you are, my lady who is filled with life's bright shining light.

Jeff To Stephanie December 7, 2007

The Picture Above

The picture above certainly looks magical doesn't it? An ethereal site in the heavens on a snowy night. Makes you think of Christmas and how it can be a special and unique time of the year. A shining time at the end of the year which creates hope for the events to come in the year to come.

I hope this Christmas will be special since the family issues are not what they were last year. I always had good memories of Christmas growing up and the time spent with my parents and extended family. My mom especially always made Christmas fun and she captured the spirit of the time for us all. Truly, I want all of our kids to gather with us and make some memories for themselves that they will treasure as they get older. I never want them to have dark remembrances of a time that I have so many light and warm memories of. Christmas is supposed to be that way, it should never be a season of woe or sadness although that is the case sometime given what life drops down the chimneys of our lives in the form of life experience presents given by fate, chance, or decisions made.

Even so, the love of family and the recollections of times together can and do compensate for times not so good times from Yuletides past. In the end it is not the physical gifts that are given that make the most difference, it is the love, compassion, and familial union that we remember the most I think. And that is what we are trying to give to our children is it not? Trying to let them know that even though we do not give them all of the physical goods they desire, they are loved regardless of their pocket books or ours for that matter.

Hopefully each succeeding Christmas we are together over the remainder of our lives will be filled with love and happy times and not just the simple desire for piles of presents under the Tree or in the stockings "hung with care" on our fireplace mantle. In that way, our children will have a wealth of good things to remember when they too one day will have a tree and dinner of their own for their children and grandchildren, perhaps mentioning what we did with (not for) them on such occasions long ago. If that does transpire one day then we did give our children the best present of them all, our love.

Jeff To Stephanie December 11, 2007

The Christmas Season

The Christmas Season is certainly upon us now my love. The excitement of this time is in the air. I, your Scrooge Husband, even feel it. There is something different about this time of the year isn't there? A time for celebration, some good food, and of course times with our family and friends. At the very least people seem to get out of the normal routines and schedules and as a culture we seem to slow our pace down some. This is a good thing I think.

We can't always be serious or so focused on work or chores. The spirit needs some playtime to remain up for the challenges that constantly present themselves to us. And I am sure we will get a new batch of them in the coming year, we always do like anyone that lives on this Earth. And so the cycle of existence will continue its spiral to who knows where in the end.

But before life sucks us back into the vortex of worry, chores, and serious matters we can enjoy the excitement of Christmas and New Year's. Being with you now for a second Christmas has made this time come more alive for me. As you know, being single I approached Christmas sometimes like an unwanted chore, outside of the family gatherings that is. But now there is a reason to be jolly. That reason is you, and our marriage which is still young. Young, bright, and shiny like the aurora in the picture. Like it, our affection for each other certainly glows and is noticed by others. It illuminates us and envelopes our life in many ways. Like the aurora overarching the sky and spreading its light to those below in some ever changing pattern. But yet in its variation there lies also lies certainty.

Yes the aurora always changes but is always there. Just as its pulsating waves of gentle light brighten the world underneath its changing celestial curve so remains our marriage which moves in its own unique pattern while still anchored in our love and why it began those months, soon to be two years, ago.

So when I am with you at this time of the calendar, in this colder season, I am yet warmed. Heated by the knowledge that we are together and we have a family. And at the same time the landscape of our life together is brightened even in dark times by the aurora of our love. Certainly, I hope others, like our children, notice its nature and perhaps see it with a sense of wonder beholding it and yet also yearning to have something like it in their own lives.

Jeff To Stephanie December 20, 2007

And the Seasons Go Round And Round

And the seasons they go 'round and 'round
And the painted ponies go up and down
We're captive on the carousel of time
We can't return we can only look behind
From where we came
And go round and round and round
In the circle game

Yes my dear I guess life is like these song lyrics by Joni Mitchell We go around and around in life, just in one direction only forward in time from somewhere behind us in the temporal progression of our existence. And to where we really do not know, only more turns of the circle can answer that question.

And what has life presented to us on this last turn? Something I'd rather not look back on per se. But yet we have to in order to make some future turn around the center of life easier. And thus things will be won't they? Maybe so, maybe not. We won't know until we get there, to some unknown state of being that we are encapsulated within, and hopefully not imprisoned by at the same time.

And life is a game in a sense is it not? We play the game, taking the hands dealt by the dealer of chance and circumstance and then respond. Sometimes there are new situations that the rules do not cover. And that is where we have nothing behind us to reference in order to see how to try to "win" the game.

In such times we are captive on the carousel you know, the events in our lives that have happened before are the only thing we can really rely on sometimes in order to decide how to react to the difficult times at hand in the present epoch of our personal geological sequence; each period of our life is but another layer, one above another deposited by the cycle of being simply alive and having relations with others like our families. And thus the carousel of time goes 'round and 'round.

And each of us, each family, has these turns of this merry-go round, these ups and downs of emotions and feelings. To what ultimate result is not really definable; everyone's life is different in some way even when they are related. But in the end the wheel turns for everyone, each generation of a family has its own set of ponies to ride to somewhere through time.

Jeff To Stephanie December 26, 2007

Another New Year Has Begun

Another New Year has begun. And we are in our second year of being married. Plus in June we will have known each other for two years. The marking of time, the noting of important mile-stones like anniversaries. These things show us where we are and where we have come from. The passage of time and of our lives is marked by these mileposts you see. The signposts on our journey through life together are these temporal markers seen on our calendars.

Certainly everyone has these events. Some people note them in different ways. People celebrate these things or simply note them quietly. Or even ignore them if there is pain associated with some date that to others is nothing in particular or something to note with happiness. So far, we have been marking our time together with celebrations even when other unhappy or difficult events swirl around the edges of our otherwise mostly idyllic existence together. I prefer to remember our important dates with happiness, not sadness or regret you see. Indeed, there are dates on the calendars of both of our lives that mark sad times or even the good and the bad all at once. Why things happen on certain dates is but either chance or the result of a decision made or a combination of such things. The date does not mark the calendar by itself, but life and our actions do.

So where we can let us always try to make the events that one day will be remembered and marked with happiness and glee. Why not try to do this since life will always try to throw us some curves? The happy times will hopefully be numerous and overshadow the bad ones. And together these days on the calendar will one day mark the time we had on this Earth and in this life, and especially in our life together as a couple.

Jeff To Stephanie January 2, 2008

Well

Well, we have been fussing some lately, and of course kissing and making up too. I was thinking about this and remember it being said that the first two years of a marriage are the hardest for a couple. Make it through that and you are on easy street.

I know that will be so with us. You made some comment one night recently that we are seeing in more detail what it is like to live with one another. I think there is a lot of truth in that statement my dear. Indeed, as we go through our days together, dealing with all of the things we get thrown at us, both good and bad, we do react to things that are part of this learning process through the lenses of our perception, colored by our being and our experiences. Sometimes these lenses are a bit blurry when it comes to seeing what the other is really doing. And this unclear sight of course causes friction with one another. After being blind for a bit so to speak we again however always see clearly and learn some more things about each other's personalities don't we?

In the end, our love and like for each other makes us veer off of the course of anger and back to the path of enjoyment, peace, and being together with one another. Many couples loose the love and like part of their relationships it seems. Maybe one sign of this is your fellow teachers never bringing their spouses to school events of whatever type. In their disdain and dislike for their mates they seek activities without them perhaps (or so we think). We do not do that of course, but always seek to be with one another regardless of the nature of things that are happening you see.

And in the end being together reminds us of why we got together in the first place perhaps. When we see each other, look into each other's eyes, or hold the other's hands, even without saying a word, we know we are connected and are a couple, even with our faults and eccentricities. Perhaps our somewhat non-typical personalities are what hold us together when others with more conventional egos and emotions seem to part ways, or live lives of being distant.

And in the end, doesn't the reality of our "on the far side of the bell curve" personalities prove why it is OK to be a bit different from everyone else we know? The proof is in the pudding of our unvarying couple-being; we are together and stay together and love each other fully and with honesty. And so it shall be, won't it?

Jeff To Stephanie January 14 2008

That Song

It has been a while since I have written one these notes to you, but after seeing the movie "Once" that we bought and hearing "that song" I feel inspired once more. Well dear, here are the lyrics to "that song" on the movie "Once". It is called "***Falling Slowly***". In short, the words are interesting and also haunting at the same time. Some of it could apply to you and me as you will probably agree. One example given some of our fusses of recent times is the phrase "Take this sinking ship and point it home. We've still got time". Etc. Certainly we have always chosen to love each other, forgive each other, and move forward to a better day. And I trust we will always do that with each other. That way we won't fall away from each other, regardless of things, as long as we are alive. So with our differences, and what we have in common, we can walk together like they are doing above.

I don't know you
But I want you
All the more for that
Words fall through me
And always fool me
And I can't react
And games that never amount

To more than they're meant
Will play themselves out
Take this sinking boat and point it home
We've still got time
Raise your hopeful voice you have a choice
You've made it now

Falling slowly, eyes that know me
And I can't go back
Moods that take me and erase me
And I'm painted black
You have suffered enough
And warred with yourself
It's time that you won

Take this sinking boat and point it home
We've still got time
Raise your hopeful voice you had a choice
You've made it now

Take this sinking boat and point it home
We've still got time
Raise your hopeful voice you had a choice
You've made it now
Falling slowly sing your melody
I'll sing along

Jeff To Stephanie March 24, 2008

Contract Day

Well dear, the die is now cast on your contract. It is like the supposed Klingon saying **"pain clarifies the mind".** In this case I guess it does. Certainly, you have endured much for no personal gain at the ISD that is for sure. The endless petty and spiteful actions perpetrated by ***"las bovinas mas gordas y mas malas y mas estupidas"*** have made a place that should have been one of opportunity for you one that was filled with daily struggles. But now, you know that wretched state of affairs will end in the foreseeable future. So it is time to move on to something better for you. And I know you will do that since your talents and qualifications are many, unlike those possessed by many of your current co-workers. But that is their problem, not yours, and now the road to a better work place is yours to drive down so to speak.

So you should strive to put your frame of mind into one that many consultants possess and one that you alluded to. See it as a contract that simply has ended and also see most of who you work with simply as unpleasant clients you will never have to deal with again. Such views will keep you sane and happy when surrounded by hordes of self-centered morons and seemingly endless series of set backs and disasters that batter the shores of your day to day work life.

And I know our fussing has not made things better either. But I know this tension will cease and we will resume our mostly happy and harmonious life together. Why? You are correct that we are right for each other. But we do need to be nicer to each other in our own ways. To get to a point where we might actually seriously think about splitting up would be a sign of two people being stupid. Instead, let us get back to where we were, the path taken by two smart people who love each other and recognize how lucky we are to have found each other in the mostly unsavory cesspool of adult dating and single life.

In short, honestly there is nothing left to fuss about, only everything to enjoy about each other and appreciate. That is my frame of mind now my dear. I do truly love you and truly and honestly look forward to spending the rest of our lives together regardless of the ups and downs caused by jobs, family, or the usual random blasts of uncertainty that life's painful guns unleash on all of us who live on this Earth.

Jeff To Stephanie March 26, 2008

Worried About My Mom

I guess I was more worried about my mom's test results than I thought in retrospect. I felt a knot in my gut all morning fearing the worst even though my "gut" told me it would all be OK. And it was OK in the end as you know.

At least this time it was all OK. It does show that we can be filled with fear, but for no major reason. Of course one does not know that until one gets to the end of the road so to speak on such things. We fear what might happen, when it is before us or not. But sometimes the worst things happen when we least expect it too.

Life is funny like that, mixing fear at odd times, and also some joy. The laughter and joy I heard in my mom and sister's voices when I talked to them this morning was that joy, and the relief of deliverance from peril. Certainly, those voices would have been different had the news been different. Of course, you and I would have dealt with another result but in this case we had good news and therefore we will have a good weekend with my mom.

One lesson, the heart of the matter of this case, is that we should be thankful for the good things we have. Our health, our kids, our family, our jobs, and of course each other my dear. While we fuss too much sometimes, thinking about something happening to you brings me back to what I should be focusing on. That is, being glad that I have you.

Yes, one day one of us will die and the one of us left on this Earth will be alone. But until that unknown day we do have each other, and that is good even if sometimes we are surrounded by life's uneven fields of sharp thorns and thistles. That is just the nature of existence whether we like it or not. But also our love is part of this reality and it should transcend the things that threaten our little realm of domestic bliss on Aransas Trail.

Jeff To Stephanie April 11, 2008

We Had A Good Weekend

We had a nice weekend indeed with my Mom didn't we? It was very good to be able to help her and spend time with her. It is obvious that she likes you and loves you especially since she told you stuff that she tells no one else but Teresa and I. Besides the obvious there also was an illustration of the continuity of family and how the generations within it move forward through time and events as they unfold.

Think back to what she spoke about. Her dad, her grandparents and other relatives removed in time and by branches of the family. All in all she told a story that actually spanned parts of three centuries: the 19th, the 20th, and the 21st. While the times changed, the actors did not since they were all Turners or Couches in some form or another. And also the things surrounding us in her place were all things I grew up with. The pictures and the furniture we sat upon all were part of earlier stories acted out before the time we met. Just as some of my furniture also consists of things I grew up with and were part of my life. And still are even though some of it now lurks in a lonely fashion in the storage place. If pieces of furniture had feelings would they feel left out when were not with us? Certainly these objects have seen the good and the bad of our family's life flow around them over the decades. These "mere" things were witness to the picture we painted on the canvass of life and existence. In the end the totality of the company (you, mom and my sister & her family), the stories, and the family belongings all made me feel comfortable…like I was home. Even though it was not where you and I make our life together.

But that is the point isn't it? That regardless of where your family lives and what the year in one's life is, family perhaps provides the most permanence in one's life. While we age and die, there are links to the past, who we are, and where we came from. Even if the links are not that many or do not go very far back as is the case with you. Regardless, they are still there in a varied and reduced form. All of us have some story to tell when asked about our family and our origins. You have one too; it just does not have the details as my lineage does. But even so, you are part of the Turner clan now. You are part of our story too, as are your children.

One day when we are old, or are already gone, our kids will be telling someone about us. Or telling someone about my mom and dad in the case of my two kiddos. Your two will have their own tales too of course; theirs will just be a bit different. Thus, over time the story of our family and its wider clan continues, with many details lost to forgetful memories, loosened ties, too many years passing, and changed circumstances, but continue it will. And thus our children will perpetuate this story and saga, adding their own tales to the wider book about this family of ours.

Jeff To Stephanie April 14, 2008

It Has Been A While

It has been a while my Stephanie Celeste since I have written you a note. Well, we have been busy with things as you know. My new job, my back ache, your job hassles, and mom's surgery. Once more life has served up a buffet of things for us to deal with, hopefully without too much experiential indigestion. And on the more happy side, getting the new cat has been a lot of fun for both of us.

So here we go now, into the second year of being a couple together my love. We have had our trials and tribulations but we both know that we love each other and marrying was the right thing for us to do. And we can look back to certain events that led to our wedding like you telling me you loved me first or our discussions of being together forever like the one by the lake watching the boat races with some cold beer. All of those times and events plot out the path that led to us being Mr. and Mrs. Turner. All of these things confirm we did the right thing and that we do belong together, regardless of how some people feel about that fact or not.

We know in our hearts that being husband and wife is a good thing and a natural thing as well.

We have no requirement to validate our feelings about each other to our extended family and its varied members, especially when they hardly seek our counsel much less approval for their life choices or lifestyles. In short we do have our own life and we do not have to justify it to anyone. We have a right to be happy with each other. And we are.

And so we continue to begin our life together Stephanie. Certainly we are a project and piece of work that will be forever in progress and not ever totally completed given our mutual levels of intelligence and somewhat quirky personalities. But that is OK with me 100%, being with you is a good thing and provides happiness, some challenges too, but also of course many levels of safety, contentment, pleasure, and security within the boundaries of our strong love for one another. So our life marches on to somewhere just like the clouds streaming over our heads, going somewhere but perhaps not knowing where exactly we will wind up. Regardless, our journey will be fun, shooting through life's atmosphere together like a band of clouds on a long journey to life's far horizons.

Jeff To Stephanie June 2. 2008

Warmth And Heat

Well Darling I have not been writing as much of these notes lately as I used to. So I feel I need to rectify that. Today, I told you about someone asking me about you in the lunch room. They inquired about you being a school teacher and I of course explained that you were and added some of your qualifications and the like. Certainly the thing I got out of that was the fact that you are a very capable woman and that I should always be proud of you, all wrapped inside of loving you, I am convinced that many people are not married to someone who is as interesting as you are.

In that analysis one can see that you are unique indeed. I should never forget that fact and I should not take those facets of your being for granted. Especially when we get into a fuss about something. Both of us should remember the things that got us together in the first place so rapidly and so intensely. Those flames of love, respect, and desire consumed us both now two years ago or so. Yes, this fiery love or ours has turned us into crispy critters of sorts but it is a satisfying type of roast isn't it? And so this conflagration of being a couple still glows and flames up too.

But of course there is a cautionary tale in all of

this. We both must always keep these fires as fires of purification, not those of consumption or incineration. The heat of this marriage of ours needs to keep us warm. And not create the type of heat that drives us away from each other. I for one would rather feel warm and snug up next to you, not singed or fried by the heat of destruction. And if we can do that for each other our relationship will always be warm even when the world outside is cold and freezing, and the snow drifts of life's struggles and trepidations march towards the doors of our home.

Jeff To Stephanie June 26, 2008

Our Talents

Your work re-modeling our kitchen made me think of something my dearest. What you ask? Specifically our different talents, some of which do not fit the usual stereotypes for what men and women usually do. Case in point is again the re-modeling. That is something you have a knack for and also enjoy. Where as I hate such things and have no natural talent for such. But on the other hand you hate cooking and have no natural ability for such things where as I do.

What this shows simply is that while we share many common interests and beliefs, you and I are not clones or even mirror images of each other. Due to our backgrounds and also our raw intelligence we are both pulled to certain things or possess certain talents. Most women would never replace an ice maker and enjoy doing it like you did. At the same time many men would never enjoy preparing a meal from scratch unless it was simply a steak or a burger. But I can do that and do not have to think about it too much.

And what does this mean for us as a couple? Well, it can mean some good things since we are both capable of many of the same things. But also I guess it opens up some doors that would not be open to us by ourselves if we were alone. Case in point is our quest for a rent house. We both know a lot about it since you are a broker and I once was. I know how to deal with tenants where as you don't. You like to fix stuff up and I don't. So that means we have a variety of skills to make the rent house quest work well for us.

I think such combinations of skills lie elsewhere in our life as a couple together. Time will make more of those become visible as we choose to do different things and as life pitches us curveballs to deal with on its playing field of uncertainty. Some couples may be more conventional in their gender-based roles but once again we deviate a bit from those seemingly normal positions. In the end I guess that is one of things that make us a good couple, albeit one that attracts some ire and curiosity from some folks who are not like us.

Jeff To Stephanie July 2, 2008

The Trip To See Jane

The trip this weekend to see Jane at A&M is certainly a sign that an era of my life has come to a close. Now that Jane is at college she truly is no longer a child or little girl. She is really now an adult and how her life turns out is largely up to her efforts, regardless of the love, support, and help we offer to her from time to time.

And that is yet no surprise and yet also a source of both gladness and sadness since the memories and images of her growing up are compared to the hopeful what ifs of her life to come in her career or path through existence. Truly we will not see her much anymore, not that we were seeing her that much as she grew older, but going off to college is a true Rubicon in life. The life of a child is gone forever and the life of an adult now begins in its truest sense. She has left home and is somewhat on her own (not entirely self sufficient but she heading that way).

And how knows where she will wind up as well? She talks about working with "the water" for her career. Now, jobs dealing with certainly are not going to be in Fort Worth, Texas you know. She very well could spend her adult life on one of the coasts or somewhere even more remote depending on what she actually winds up doing.

This yin and yang experience of a child that one loves growing up certainly applies to all of our other three kids too. Roger, Jimmy, and Cynthia all have or are making these same transitions as you know. They all are making different choices, some we understand, some we do not, and some we do not agree with, but choosing their own paths they are doing even now.

And they will continue doing so since at this time in our lives we are mostly watching the drama that is their lives. We can just turn on life's TV so to speak and watch another episode, sometimes we will do more than watch, but for the most part that will not be the case. As parents we want to guide, protect, and sometimes chastise our kids, but that time in life is very nearly over now. While we are loved by our kids, they will forever now be somewhat or mostly apart and distant from us by the very nature of their adult existence.

Even Jimmy and Cynthia who both live very close to us are not around much for they have their own lives now; we cannot be part of our kid's lives as we once were. Even my mom and I, and Teri, do not see each other all of the time like we did in years gone by.

And I do now better understand why my mom

wants to see me and Teri. Like us missing our brood, she simply misses us and can still picture us as little kids who have yet to grow up, get independent, and leave the nest. Thus, this distance is a fact of life and something we all have to adjust to. While sometimes gut wrenching and melancholy by its nature it is also something to be happy about as we see our kids find their own ways through things as we did, and still do. That in and of itself is something to enjoy as we hopefully see our kids find happiness and a path through their own world and lives.

Jeff To Stephanie September 2, 2008

The Sadness One Feels

The sadness one feels when you see a child growing up and knowing that seeing him or her will be something ever more infrequent is something that makes an impression on you. Last Monday when we told Jane bye at Galveston I had one of those moments. There she was 18 years old and starting college in a town 300 miles from home. Sure with cell phones and email one can easily stay touch with someone at a distance but that is not the same as being able to see them. Seeing her all grown up made me think about how she looked as a little girl too. And changing over the years into the pretty young lady that she is now. Remember that picture I have of her in our office upstairs I took when she was about eight of her out in the field at Granbury with her arms outstretched and smiling so hugely in a grand pose on that winter day? That image of her exuberance and being filled with life without worries will be how I always remember her.

I think most parents do that, they will always try to think of their kids as little when they are innocent and have not learned the various ways of adults that many times are not so innocent you know. Thinking of them that way perhaps we as adults long for a life that is a fairy tale. We want an existence that always has a happy ending and where everyone is good and all acts are decent. But we know that is not the case in life. In our family we see our relatives and our children sometimes doing things that while not evil or bad per se certainly do not fit the stereotype of good that we see in fables and fairy tales. Certainly the yin of reality contrasts with the yang of what we wish life would be like.

And it is a yin and yang thing. A child growing up and embarking on life's journey as a grown up finally is a good and natural thing. A good parent should rejoice that their children can take on the challenges of life and build their own life and one day and have a good and loving family of their own. That should be the natural progression of life if all is well. We cannot as parents expect to be there everyday with our grown up kids. That would be unnatural and hinder their own maturation process. But yet even with the knowledge that a child now is grown and has their own life we again think back to when they were little and needed us. That push and pull of emotions is what makes a time of transition from child to young adult hard on us parents who now remain at homes that are quieter now that the children have left. Perhaps the new found silence is one thing that makes us think more about our kids. Now that there are fewer distractions there is more time for contemplation. Which sometimes results in the sadness of seeing one's kids only in memories ever more often.

So at this stage in our lives it seems that we are not needed per se, perhaps we are wanted sometimes, as our children mature. But regardless we still have the images deep inside of our minds of what were our now grown kids when they were little and so full of life, happiness, good, and hope for what was ahead of them, saved up for those days when those very same individuals, those we love, may try us.

Jeff To Stephanie September 3, 2008

Surprises And Such

Well, well, well. The election will be resolved and the end of the campaign draws neigh. Thank goodness, I have truly grown sick of it, especially the media and its near orgasmic tilt for Senator Obama. But this painful process illustrates that regardless of the ups and downs of our political culture life pretty much goes on as it always does. And so does our life in general. Like last Saturday's surprise trip to the hospital with Jimmy. You never know what will happen. One minute things are good or in the usual routine and then the polarity of life's electrical circuits switch in a sudden reversal creating worry and angst. Darkness where a minute ago there was light and clarity.

So like the sun rising and setting, changing light to dark and dark back into light our lives are ultimately set by these rhythms every day and year. But not on a regular schedule like the sun however. The uncertainty of when both good things and bad things take place provides one with a certain amount of variety, much of it unwanted, some of it necessary, and some of it a source of joy.

Jimmy's trip to the hospital is certainly one

example of an unwanted but also necessary event. And yet one which would not have happened quite the same way unless we had not met in the first place. Good begets bad in way you know. To be sure Jimmy's getting sick that day most likely would have happened if we had never met and married but how it transpired would have been different had I not been in your life, and certainly I would have never known about it with you absent from my existence. But I was there and I was able to get Jimmy in the truck and get him to the hospital. So in the end something good came out of that bad situation: I was able to be there for him and you too.

So life's uncertain events are certainly not a clockwork sunrise but more of an inconstant moon in the skies of our lives. Each day we awake and find out what will be served up to us, sometimes an un-tasty buffet, but also sometimes a welcome and joyous feast. Regardless, these things define the uncertain pattern of our lives.

Jeff to Stephanie November 4. 2008

Christmas And Material Gifts

Christmas and material gifts. You know your email this morning made me think of how we usually celebrate Christmas. That is the centrality of gift giving in our culture within the circle of the holiday and all it is about or supposed to be about. In most public venues one hears mostly about getting stuff, or buying stuff at the cheapest price possible to give to others. For the most part little is heard on the public airwaves about how Christmas started or how family is involved in it. It does seem that the voices saying that Christmas is too commercial are right.

Now you and I are not the most religious people in the world but we do see beyond what the material culture states the holiday is about. You said all you wanted for Xmas was me, and I replied the same back to you. In our statements to each other we eschewed the act of giving stuff and instead gave each other love back and forth. When you look at the ultimate result of the traditional Christian Christmas message love ***is*** the answer. That is, Xmas is supposed to be about the birth of Jesus: The Father "who so ***loved*** the world that he begat his only son". Ignoring the dogma and doctrine of mainline Christianity one can see that Western culture has for the most part forgotten the basis for this holiday and ultimately what it should mean to people. That is love and caring should be above accumulating more and more "stuff" and that ultimately sacrificing for one's family is perhaps the supreme virtue.

Therefore, at this time of year, and of course on Turkey Day, the gatherings of family should be about the family and it being together. Not about how much did we spend on presents or what is in the stockings over our fireplace. It should be about being a family group, even with its periodic issues and difficulties. We should be glad that life itself, not Santa or some unseen God, gave us each other and that most of the time we love one another and not love the stuff we give others in our circle or possess individually.

Perhaps if we did that more each Yuletide season our kids and one day their descendents might get a better idea about the things that are more permanent and transcend mere material goods that break and are discarded when their use is done. It is true families and especially our lives are also not permanent, but the holiday times together and their related traditions and memories are what we hold dear and define mileposts in our lives. They also create tales that we pass on to those in generations after our own. And thus some of what we are and were will influence the lives of those who will come after us. That truly is a gift worth giving even when those that receive it from us may not be at the stage of their own lives to appreciate the value of this and see beyond the transient and specious nature of mere belongings.

Jeff To Stephanie December 10, 2008

Christmas Family Gathering Angst

Xmas Family Gathering Angst. Well in the end we are set it seems to get the Turner clan (comprised of its various family branch components: Turner, Long, Gray, and Garnett) together. True, I got somewhat stressed about it while trying to nail everyone down as to when we would at least attempt to initiate the familial Yuletide conclave. And again, it is all set up now and everyone knows when it will be and what we will be eating while we are together.

But back again to angst. It does seem that each Christmas and Thanksgiving we have seen as a couple there has been some turmoil. Especially our first holiday season together when everyone shunned us. Well, not being love struck teenagers we really did not need anyone's blessing to marry. But I digress on that. Outside of the strife of our initial marrying, there still has been at least some logistical stress when trying to make sure we continued our tradition of holiday feasting as a family.

And now the source of this less than pleasing condition. As we have talked about it before it is the change in family patterns due to the changes in the phase of life the family is in. Now, everyone is grown, the younger ones are off at college or working. And those of us in the middle: you, me, my sister, and Scott find that it is difficult to reconcile everyone's different schedules and lives so that the whole bunch of us are at one place at a time. And now my mom, who used to be in the middle, largely comes as me or my sister decides the time and place to gather. This state of affairs will never get any simpler. As our kids marry and have their own kids, and move perhaps far away from us, the times the whole family gathers will certainly be fewer.

Certainly this is universal to most families in our "mobile society". Even in the Greater Turner Clan this is true: I cannot remember the last time we got with the Calhouns on a holiday occasion. We probably will not ever do that again due to the reality of all of our lives. And the Couch gatherings were long ago permanently relegated to my memories alone due to the lasting bad feelings of "The Mess".

And therein lays some sadness at least for me. As you have heard many times, I do have many fond memories of family get-togethers, at least from my childhood. Recalling those events, stretching back now some decades into the past century, they certainly are still with me in my mind and in my emotions. From smoked turkey to being in Valley

View with mom's family and then going across Lee Street to my dad's family, these events defined in many ways what I think a family is and how it should behave. So when current events do not meet that certainly now idealistic remembrance of those times part of me is left aching, sometimes sad, and perhaps longing for the fantasy like return of what I saw when I was a kid. Maybe most people are like that. When some difficulty arises in the present we hark back to some Norman Rockwell like vision of our past to seek comfort and reassurance that things are well.

One way or the other, I hope our times together paint some "Norman Rockwell's" for our children that they can recall in the coming years and decades when their own lives become complicated like ours seems to be sometimes. And in any event, Merry Christmas my love, may it be merry in spite of any difficulties that this season brings to us. And may the Christmases that lie ahead of us in life also be happy and jolly.

Jeff To Stephanie December 23, 2008.

Another Year Is Upon Us

Another new year is upon us. And what does it mean? The usual thing our culture expects us to feel is excitement in order to set the stage for the New Year to be better than the last one. Sometimes when one year is not so good that is easier said than done. But yet year after year we are presented with the same mind numbing and sometimes nauseating message of happiness and goodwill to come. Of course the masses love this, as evidenced by annually repeated idiocy like "the ball" being dropped in New York in Times Square, itself teeming with drunken legions of urban lemmings congregated in a huge moving and intoxicated mass in front of live TV.

And as the years march past my eyes I care less and less for such hoopla. Even Christmas has lost most of its excitement and magic as you know. And why has this happened? Is it just a fact of getting older and having now seen dozens of these annual rituals? All of them blurring into a fog of past memories fading into the void of approaching elderly forgetfulness? Or is it because many of these events were not filled with Norman Rockwall like jolliness and glee that we are supposed to expect to be present?

Most likely it is a combination of both of these things I think. After a half a century of Christmases just what has to happen to make the next one really stand out from the many that have already passed by? And how many seasonal gatherings can be marred by some family issue before one starts to associate these times with such unpleasantness? Just in the time we have been together I think we could say we have seen both sets of conditions show up on our life's stage to perform a less than well reviewed play, perhaps even a Greek tragedy of sorts? Certainly our first Christmas was not filled with widespread joy that is for sure.

But perhaps I am just getting more cynical. However now, this last Christmas was not so bad, the gathering on the 27th was pretty fun and no one fussed or thought they were being ignored by some other family faction. Thus in a way there has been some redemption for the holiday season that forgave its painful past times and its past sins, or the things we perceived as such. In that way I guess the sometimes less than happy memories of times long ago will be lessened and the hope for better times will in fact be renewed in our hearts as our lives unfold across the rough and uncharted sea of the future that is the very nature human existence.

Jeff To Stephanie December 31, 2008

The Other Side Of the Sky

Well, seeing Jane so sad when we left Galveston made me sad too. As I said driving back it has been a long time since I saw that look on her face. She is usually a pretty happy young lady and full of life. But at her dorm she certainly looked like life had been sucked out of her. So with her Sad-Sack eyes we hugged her bye and climbed in the truck and turned for home.

Once we left Galveston did you notice that there was a shield of cirrus clouds stretching from the southwest to the northeast? It originated some where southwest of Houston and flowed northeast with the jet stream. On the top of the causeway with the clear sky the filaments of these ice clouds arched over the Earth stretching back to the western horizon and beyond. The clarity of the air made the clouds stand out sharply over the land of the coastal plain, its own features visible in such crisp relief that one could see the surface slope up to the rolling terrain beyond in the far distance.

And as time and miles unfolded we were underneath it for a while. Then once we were nearly to Waco we were on the other side of it. As we drove further north away from Jane and closer to home, I kept looking in the rear view mirror at those clouds, still arching over one far horizon to another.

Perhaps you thought I was just checking the traffic, but my gaze was looking far beyond what was just behind us. And while this visage was of course very beautiful, I still kept thinking of Jane, sitting alone in her dorm room on the other side of that sky. The clouds represented crossing a Rubicon: a divide in time and one's life. We had crossed it, so had Jane, and the past of was course gone forever as she took one more step in her adult life being at college far from home pursuing her own dreams and not being that smiling little girl standing in a field in the picture on my desk.

I guess our lives are many times like this. The past is always on the other side of life's sky, not ever to be the same again. Just as clouds flow overhead never looking the same, and vanish in the distance, our memory of past events fades over time as they recede ever further from the present.

So, when you gaze outside on a day like yesterday, and a web of cirrus spreads across the sky, you should remember that there are some times people who are dear to our hearts far away on the other side of those airy wisps, perhaps also looking up at those same clouds towards us and thinking of home, family, and being loved.

Jeff To Stephanie, January 19, 2009

A Child's Frustration's

Roger called me today. He got an answer of sorts back on whether or not the college would let him take the substitute class or not. They told him they would make a decision but the counselor told him since he made a pretty good grade in his last remedial math class they might make him take a regular class. Well, not hearing first hand all of the details I cannot say what his choices are. But he was very frustrated and wanted to hear something from me to give him direction or comfort. He wanted to tell his Dad what was wrong. I felt sad for him, and I wanted to help him but I really could not do that given the nature of this beast. But one cannot escape or forget the feelings one has for their children, the parent of long ago, the one that picked up a crying little kid, is still there aching to help the now grown man or woman. But helping is not something that is always possible or desirable. But it is a feeling that nonetheless exists in a good parent's heart and soul.

In summary I told him to make an appointment with the department head to get some final ruling on what he needed to do get his degree. And he was OK with that. But that is not the point of what I am writing about here. What the true point is that simply here was my son who was upset and wanting to talk to me about something that was important to him and his life. His way of reaching out is not the same as Jane's as you know.

But he did reach out and he was not blaming me for anything. He was simply saying he was tired of trying so hard just to keep having setbacks put in front of him. In the end he of course has to find a solution since he is a grown up, I cannot do it for him. That is certainly one of life's harsh lessons. One must ultimately chart one's course through the harsh and rough seas of existence.

Hopefully to some safe harbor. But unfortunately there are reefs and shoals lurking beneath even the calmest seas of one's life that can wreck the ship sailing one's desired course.

Now this all happened during the work day, I went outside on lunch to call him back. No idyllic clouds or bright sunshine on this child's problems. Just everyday reality framing it into sharp focus. In that lies another one of life's truths. Every day is different than the last, and every person and child is different. They have their own characteristics and features. All rolled up into something individual and unique. And that is what colors our lives. The good and the bad envelope us every day, every month, and every year that we are on this Earth. In the end, perhaps this is the one thing all of us must learn and be willing to deal with so that we remain happy, and sane enough to face each day's challenges. And be there for our loved ones, and of course for ourselves, when difficult times and woes challenge us.

Jeff To Stephanie January 20, 2009.

Disappointment

Well I know you are disappointed in what happened today in your interview. That is a natural thing especially when you do know what you are doing and your skills are very high. Again, it seems "they" do not seem to recognize what you do for the ISD and allude to things in your personality. One really asks "why do I try so hard"? When one works very hard and is good at one's calling it is a very real let down to not have that hard work show some better benefit than what one has in the present.

I have felt that same way many times in my career, the very same. And I too run in to it again as you seem to do. And so the cycle continues, and continues to frustrate our beings. At times like that I think about doing something totally different for work and a paycheck. I think I keep seeing the same old set of problems and issues over and over again just in a different setting and place. But the reality of earning the same income then rears its ugly head and keeps me in this line of work.

I wish one day we would not have those constraints and we could try something different without it bankrupting us and making it hard to take care of things or help our kids. Perhaps one way to make this dream and desire come true to is to try a little step. Like me trying to build the books of The Notes to you. Maybe if I am lucky it will sell a lot and could mean the freedom to write more things like it. Or maybe not of course. Regardless it is worth a try, at least until we win the Lottery of course. Well the Lotto is a fantasy but the books may not be.

And what should you do my dearest? I am not sure but since you and I are in many ways alike, perhaps finding a new path is the solution for you as well. That exact path of course is for you to decide and formulate. Perhaps the only true answer to this question comes from within alone. And then acting in some reasonable manner to try to achieve it. Time alone will tell what happens but at least thinking about such things is a start that many people never attempt to do. And maybe therein lays our ultimate salvation that at least we can think of something outside of our normal routine and hope for something better than just the same old paycheck and problems.

Jeff To Stephanie January 20, 2009

The Ghost Of Love Past

In the past two days we have seen both of my two kids, they are yours too you know, feel upset about something important in their lives. In both cases I too have felt sad due to their personal sadness. And in both cases I have responded to them, of course in different ways since they are different people with unique personalities and situations. As I wrote the other day, as a parent I want to "make it all better", but I cannot do that all of the time. It is very true that I remember them both as if they were little kids again. Innocent, full of love and full of life's experiences which at a young age are mostly full of wonder and excitement. Of course they are both young adults now but the ghosts of their childhood haunt me it seems.

Much of this emotion comes from knowing they are grown now and also from not having them around. Per se I do not suffer from "empty nest syndrome" but in a way perhaps I do. One's happy memories of for example taking them to the park and watching them play are always somewhere in my sub-conscious mind. These fond remembrances are present; such things fill your mind too. Knowing that these times will not replay themselves is something that one knows but at the same time perhaps wants to reject the obvious reality of.

The reason is simple. As a loving parent our kids are always there in our minds and hearts. Maybe they are not always in the forefront of our thoughts but they always color our feelings. Even when these long ago images are far below the waves of the sea of our conscious minds. Thus, when things happen to them that remind us that they are adults our minds, anchored in the past, want to revolt against this fact and thus we are saddened.

I can fully understand now why my mom is the way she is. She always was there for me and my sister. And let us not forget my dad as well. And she still is when times get rough even though we of course sometimes do not see eye to eye. Regardless of the occasional enmity, she still is a loving mom. She always will be. I hope our kids will see us the same way over the coming years especially when we are gone from this life. Certainly she still sees us as little as we once were. It is only natural to do so.

In your case, you really never had a true family but yet you have the same type of attachment and love for your two kids, they are mine as well, that caused you to care so very much. I think that the fact that you were an orphan made you love your kids even more, giving them what you did not have as a child. You are a very loving mother that is certain. And it shows in the angst you sometimes feel about "your two". If you did not I would be worried about you (and if I did not you should be worried about me). Perhaps this shows that all of us, regardless of our backgrounds as kids, have the capacity to love our children as they grow up.

So one can see I think that it is a natural thing for one to love their kids, even when they are grown. As we can never forget who they were when they were little so can we also not forget that they are grown up now like us. Our love remains for them but how we express that love is different since they and us are at different points on life's road. And that we must always remember and is something they too will learn one day when they are parents.

Jeff To Stephanie January 21, 2009

Afterward

The Ghost of Love Past was the last ILYPANTS I wrote. There are no more of them. Why? With great disappointment we got divorced a little short of our third anniversary. As we fussed, I wrote fewer and fewer of them. One can perhaps see the signs of this in some of the notes. As a result of the divorce I changed the names of everyone, except mine, to somewhat protect everyone's privacy. Thus, "Stephanie" is not her name.

Regardless of the end of our marriage when I read through these notes they certainly show how our life together was on many days. They are filled with words and events that still fill me with a variety of emotions arising from those still sharp, and sometimes bittersweet, memories. And they should do that. If they did not make me feel something then I would not be human after all. Thus, when you read them I hope they fill you with those same things I feel: happiness, hope, dread, excitement, love, and the other emotions that being alive provides us whether or not they are good, bad, or something in between. Such is our existence as individuals, couples, and families

www.ingramcontent.com/pod-product-compliance
Lightning Source LLC
Chambersburg PA
CBHW031508270326
41930CB00006B/306

* 9 7 8 0 6 1 5 3 2 3 5 2 7 *